Organising a
Conference

How To Books are designed to help people achieve their goals. They are for everyone wishing to acquire new skills, develop self-reliance, or change their lives for the better. They are accessible, easy to read and easy to act on.
Other titles in the series include:

Effective Problem Solving
How to understand the process and practise it successfully

Making Effective Speeches
How to motivate and persuade in every business situation

Managing Meetings
How to prepare, how to take part and how to follow up effectively

Managing Successful Teams
How to achieve your objectives by working effectively with others

Managing Your Time
What to do and how to do it in order to do more

Writing a Report
A step-by-step guide to report writing

The *How To Series* now contains
nearly 250 titles in the following categories:

Business & Management
Computer Basics
General Reference
Jobs & Careers
Living & Working Abroad
Personal Finance
Self-Development
Small Business
Student Handbooks
Successful Writing

For full details, please send for a free copy of the latest catalogue to:

How To Books
Plymbridge House, Estover Road
Plymouth PL6 7PZ, United Kingdom
Tel: 01752 202301   Fax: 01752 202331
www.howtobooks.co.uk

Organising a
Conference

*How to plan and run
an outstanding and effective event*

PAULINE APPLEBY

How To Books

First published in 1999 by
How To Books Ltd, 3 Newtec Place,
Magdalen Road, Oxford OX4 1RE. United Kingdom.
Tel: (01865) 793806. Fax: (01865) 248780.
email:info@howtobooks. co.uk
www.howtobooks.co.uk

British Library Cataloguing in Publication Data
A catalogue record for this book is available from
the British Library

Cover design by Shireen Nathoo Design

Produced for How To Books by Deer Park Productions
Typeset by PDQ Typesetting, Stoke-on-Trent, Staffs.
Printed and bound by Cromwell Press, Trowbridge, Wiltshire

NOTE: The material contained in this book is set out in good
faith for general guidance and no liability can be accepted
for loss or expense incurred as a result of relying in particular
circumstances on statements made in the book. The laws and
regulations may be complex and liable to change, and readers
should check the current position with the relevant authorities
before making personal arrangements.

Contents

List of Illustrations

Preface

I recently attended a planning meeting for a large conference to be run by a national animal welfare charity. In addition to the national conference in which I was to be involved, each of the regional managers was also to organise a smaller conference in their own region. The questions they asked me in relation to their individual events were ones commonly asked by people in similar positions, i.e. those required to organise a conference for which they have little or no experience.

This guide is written with those people in mind. It may be that having read it you become aware of how much work is involved and either decide that you do have the time, ability and resources available to do it yourself, or identify it as a project to be out-sourced. A common result is for a combination of these two outcomes, where some elements of the organisational task are handled in-house, whilst others are out-sourced to professionals.

Of course, all organisers have their own way of doing things and the message must be to find what works for you and to learn by all of your experiences, be they as a delegate or as an organiser.

I would like to acknowledge the help and advice of the following friends and colleagues whose opinions I value very much: Monica Allen, Jayne Buckland, Caroline Hannon, Deborah Delord, Tracey Johnson, Malcom Thompson (MC Productions) and Peter Worger (ACE).

Lastly, not only do I hope you will find this guide useful, but also that you enjoy what you do.

Pauline Appleby

1

What is a Conference?

UNDERSTANDING THE REASONS FOR CONFERENCES

The *Oxford Dictionary* defines a conference as a meeting for discussion. Conferences are sometimes also called seminars, which are usually smaller groups of delegates, or symposiums – a conference or meeting to discuss a particular subject. Whatever the title, and whatever the subject, one thing is instrumental to them all: that is *communication*.

From the local gardening club to the richest charities, from trade associations to multinational companies, all will have their own agenda and reason for running a conference. It could be:

- for fund-raising
- to raise awareness
- to share information
- a learning forum
- a promotional event
- to bring together members or employees spread throughout the country or overseas.

Very different reasons and very different organisations, but there are many elements of the organisation process of the event that will be similar in each case.

Knowing who runs conferences

Some organisations employ dedicated conference staff, often within an events department, trained by staff experienced in event management. This is often the case if the organisation runs several events each year as part of the company's overall marketing strategy. Freelance professional conference organisers may be contracted-in to increase manpower when required. Alternatively, in these days of short-term contracts and tendering, an organisation may contract-out all of their event management to a freelance organiser or specialist company. This can be beneficial to the company as a cost-effective option allowing the company to concentrate on its core skills and objectives.

However in many, particularly smaller, organisations, charities, societies and clubs, the responsibility for putting together the conference is often delegated to an untrained and inexperienced person, committee member or marketing assistant who is expected to take on the workload whilst carrying out their normal job.

> **A well run conference belies the amount of work that is carried out in preparation.**

Indeed the task can be a daunting one, and there are many pitfalls, but with guidance it can be done. A well organised event can have a great impact on the stakeholders, be they paying delegates, invited guests, speakers, members of the press, in-house staff etc, but a badly organised event can have a disastrous effect which will be remembered for a long time. Many professional conference organisers originally came into the industry 'unintentionally' having been asked to run their first conference whilst working in other roles. Having enjoyed it so much they then chose to make a career move into the industry.

UNDERSTANDING THE IMPORTANCE OF COMMUNICATION

Communication is vital to society. Without communication we would have no chance of survival. The very fact that early man was a co-operative hunter means that they must have been able to communicate in one way or another. A crying baby communicates its feelings of hunger by crying, a board of directors communicates with shareholders by written communication, a mute person communicates using hand signals. To impart information of any kind we need to find the method of communication appropriate to our circumstances.

Conferences are all about communication – be it to sell, to inform, to enthuse, to entertain, or to educate.

Types of communication

Many different methods of communication are used. The first we normally think of is of course verbal, but the first communication you have with a delegate will probably be in the form of written words. During the event itself messages will be received, sometimes subliminally, by the delegates through:

- logos
- diagrams
- banners
- body language (facial expressions, body posture and gestures).

As the conference manager you must be aware of the need for good communication skills. Think of all the people you will be interacting with. A few are shown in Figure 1.

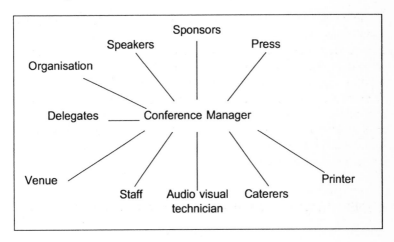

Fig. 1. Communicating as conference manager.

How you already interact

You will already be communicating with many people in your own organisation, whether they are work colleagues or fellow society members. Think about the various groups who you interact with on a regular basis. Try drawing a diagram as Figure 1, and include as many groups as possible and list below each which types of communication you may use. You will be surprised at how many there are and so how practiced you must already be!

GETTING TO KNOW THE CONFERENCE INDUSTRY

The conference industry itself is substantial and growing. It includes a vast number of different job functions including the following people. Although you will not necessarily need to involve all of them in your event, you will inevitably work with at least some.

Understanding the different job functions

Audio visual companies
Suppliers of **audio visual** equipment. They can also provide stage sets, lighting, autocues, lecterns, microphones, etc. Many also offer a service of producing computer generated presentations and other visual aids to your requirements.

Set builders
Suppliers and installers of stage sets built to your own specification.

Speakers
Conveyors of the message of your conference. Very important people!

Caterers
Providers of refreshments during the event. They may be in-house, or contracted in.

Venue-finding companies
Manage databases of all kinds of venues around the country (and overseas), and will find and negotiate with venues to suit your budget and requirements.

Venue staff
From front of house staff, security officers, to co-ordinators – all have a role to play.

Graphic designers
Producers of signs, banners, stage dressings and much more.

Printers
For production of brochures, sales literature, programmes, etc.

Mailing houses
To handle brochure mailings and to provide databases.

Badge production companies
Produce ranges of badges to suit requirements.

Registration companies
To provide delegate registration services before and/or during the event.

Crèche
To provide child care facilities enabling mothers (and fathers) to attend the event when they otherwise might not be able to.

Partnership programme organisers
To provide entertainment for delegates' partners for duration of the event.

Transcribing services
To convert verbal presentations to a readable format.

Interpreters
To translate presentations for foreign visitors/speakers.

Hoteliers
Providing a wide range of hotel accommodation with conference facilities.

Chairperson
To perform the important task of introducing speakers and providing a link between them.

Lighting suppliers
To provide lighting rigs and technicians to your own specifications.

Technicians
To operate the audio visual equipment, etc.

PLANNING YOUR OWN CONFERENCE

Conferences can be customised to your own specific requirements.

They can last for a whole day, half a day, a weekend, an evening, two days or more. The word 'conference' merely describes the nature of the event. The content, duration and outcome of it can be entirely at your discretion. Although you may feel more confident following someone else's example at your first event, feel free to be imaginative and creative. Conferences do not all have to consist of a panel of speakers addressing a totally passive audience. You could include debates, hands-on experiences, workshops and discussion groups. It can be kicked off with a sponsored breakfast and finished off with a gala dinner. You can incorporate a small exhibition, a competition or challenge of some kind, and utilise lighting, special effects and imaginative stage sets to increase the impact of the event.

Individualising your conference
Conferences can be held in hotels, on boats, in museums, in purpose-built conference and training centres. They can be for half a dozen people or for thousands. They may be run in conjunction with a major exhibition, or they may be a conference first and foremost and include their own small exhibition. No two events are the same, not even when run by the same organisation on the same theme. The mix of speakers, organisers, delegates and supporting staff will combine to produce a different atmosphere every time. External events attracting media interest in a particular subject can vastly increase the popularity of the event if the interest is positive, or drastically affect its success if negative.

Fees charged for attending events vary enormously. Some events are free of charge, whilst others may charge hundreds of pounds for a one-day event. Budgets may be huge, supported by big sponsorship deals, or it may be run on a shoe-string and be self-financing.

There may be one or two speakers, or there may be dozens. Speakers may be paid hundreds of pounds, or just expenses. Every organiser will have their own way of doing things, their own priorities and their own schedule. You will need to find what works for you.

Benefits of a conference
- Provides an environment for networking.

- Provides a forum for discussion.

- Provides an opportunity to promote ideas/products/beliefs.

- Creates a sense of belonging.

- Can enable learning and awareness.

CHECKLIST

- What resources are available to you and what happens if you need more?

- What are the limits of your responsibilities and what tasks can you delegate? Don't forget you can delegate authority but you cannot delegate responsibility.

- What can you, and what would you like to, do yourself?

- What do you need help to do?

- What contacts do you already have? Where can you find more?

- What help is available?

- How many different purposes can you list for your conference?

CASE STUDIES

Sue's trade association plans a national conference

Sue works as an assistant to the marketing manager in a trade organisation. The members of the association are based throughout the UK and do not have the opportunity to network very often. The chief executive has decided that an annual conference would be in order, to enable the members to discuss items of particular interest to them all, to review the progress and implications of forthcoming legislation, and to enable members in different parts of the country to meet and exchange ideas. The event will run over two days and will include an evening of entertainment and socialising.

The association management will be suggesting possible speakers but it is Sue's responsibility to organise and manage the event on site.

Andy's charity is to run motivating regional events

Andy is one of four regional representatives working for an animal welfare charity at a regional centre. The centres are funded mostly by volunteers who give up their time to raise money to help rehabilitate abused and abandoned animals. It has been decided to run a conference in each region featuring a well known fund-raising guru to help maximise their effectiveness and motivation for the task. Its secondary aim is to instil a feeling of 'belonging' so that their loyalty to the charity remains strong.

Andy and the other three regional representatives have each been provided with a budget and asked to organise the event in their own area.

Jean is tasked with organising a conference to promote a research paper

Jean works in the public relations department of a university. One of the university departments is about to publish a high-profile research paper that will have positive implications for the UK automotive industry and will create much media interest in the university. In order to make the most of this opportunity the Chancellor of the university has asked the public relations department to organise a conference where the paper will be presented. Local and national media are to be invited, as well as potential financial investors and sponsors from industry.

2

Choosing a Venue

LOOKING AT YOUR OPTIONS

More often than not delegates will be attending a conference in order to learn something and/or to exchange information.

> **The more the organisers can do to create an
> ideal learning environment the better.**

This does not mean the provision of schoolmasters and blackboards, but an environment as comfortable and distraction-free as possible. Delegates arriving after perhaps a long and testing journey need to be able to enter a calm atmosphere, and be able to relax and shut out the outside world. The venue, its location, and the demeanour of the conference and venue staff all have a large part to play in this.

Choosing the venue to suit your budget

Conference venues come in all shapes and sizes with varying facilities and with equally varied budgets.

- Modern, purpose-built conference centres have the latest in audio visual equipment.

- Training centres belonging to large corporations are leased out when not in use.

- Country houses offer numerous outdoor activities within their grounds.

- Hotels have the benefit of overnight accommodation and sometimes leisure facilities for delegates.

If you are working on a tight budget, civic centres and council-owned buildings such as sports and leisure centres can be a very economical option. In these venues the charge is often based upon room hire cost and the catering is supplied by an outside caterer who retains a contract with the council. The facilities will vary from very basic sports halls to grand Victorian council chambers.

Making use of universities

Universities offer a choice of conference facilities at a reasonable cost. These can vary from basic lecture theatres with hard wooden benches and graffiti-covered desks (thankfully more of a rarity these days) to state-of-the-art, purpose-built conference suites with individual cushioned seating. A major advantage of university facilities is that during the vacation periods the student accommodation can be booked at an extremely reasonable price. Again, the standard of this accommodation can vary enormously from university to university.

Considering somewhere unusual

Other more unusual venues include football and horse-racing stadiums. Again, these often offer excellent value for money and due to the nature of their core business have superb car parking and dining facilities, and are often well signposted on roads in the surrounding area. Museums can also provide a venue with a difference. Having refreshments on a gallery overlooking a display of dinosaur skeletons can provide unexpected but much appreciated interest for the delegates, and their often tiered theatres can be of a very high standard.

- For an very unusual event, why not charter a boat and have your conference whilst floating sedately down a river?

MAKING SENSE OF THE BROCHURE

Almost every conference facility will produce a leaflet or brochure describing their facilities to would-be organisers. Remember that the purpose of providing this information is to present the venue in the best possible light, so use the information purely as a guideline on which to base your further enquiries.

Knowing what to look for

Whether you are booking a four star hotel, a leisure centre or a university complex the brochure should give you:
- contact information
- an overview of the venue itself

- room capacity according to layout required.

Use the information wisely – a room capacity of 100 delegates may be fine if front projection is being used, but for back projection that number could reduce dramatically. A hall advertised as being suitable for 200 delegates may appear at first glance to look perfect, until you realise that those delegates are going to have to share two toilets during the 15-minute coffee break.

- Use your brochure to short-list the venues that *appear* suitable.

ASSESSING VENUE-FINDING OPTIONS

In every town there will be dozens of potential venues, with capacities varying from ten people to 1,000. So how do you know where to start looking?

Venue-finding services

Professional venue-finding services can be found listed in *Yellow Pages* directories and in trade journals (see Further Reading). They can dramatically cut down the time and money you need to spend on making initial enquiries. The service is usually free as they are financed by commission payable when the client makes the booking. It is likely that they will have a wealth of knowledge about different types of venues, and will usually locate a selection of potential venues for you to view. Often they will arrange for a brochure to be sent to you and make appointments for viewing on your behalf.

Considering the pros and cons of using a venue-finding service

- Sometimes the choice of venues on their books is limited to those who pay to be there, which can mean that the service may be biased.

- Venue-finding services will also often negotiate costs with venues on your behalf. They will already have a good idea of how far below the published delegate price a particular venue is likely to go.

Venue-finding software

There are various software packages on the market, some of which are available free of charge, from which you can download onto your own computer a short-list of potentially suitable venues. Again these may be limited to the companies who pay to have their information included but the choice is extensive.

Using a local council conference bureau

Most local councils now have dedicated conference departments, usually attached to the tourism bureau, whose job it is to attract conferences and events to their area. The standard of service varies enormously, from simply providing brochures to arranging hosted visits, arranging partner programmes and making hotel bookings. The staff can be less biased than privately run venue-finding services as they are not subject to private financing. The British Association of Conference Destinations produces an excellent handbook containing contact details of its members (see Useful Addresses).

Advice

No matter how suitable a venue looks from the brochure, do try to visit. Even if you will find it difficult finding the time to travel to another part of the country, it will be well worth making the effort. You could always take the train and work while you travel!

VIEWING A POTENTIAL VENUE

It is essential to book an appointment before visiting a venue so that your point of contact is able to devote his/her time to you. Arrive a few minutes early to enable you to assess your own first impression of the facility. Imagine you are a delegate, entering for the first time. Remember that in the role of organiser you are going to get to know the building and staff very well before and during the event, but your delegates will pretty much take the venue at face value for their shortened stay.

Observing the staff

Sit back and observe how the staff interact with each other.

- Are they cheerful and respectful of one another, or is there underlying discontent?
- How are they dealing with other visitors to the venue?

Before you visit, draw up a list of the essential items that you will require for your particular event. These are items that cannot be compromised upon, however much you are impressed with the venue. Also take a checklist of general items, such as the one in Figure 2, so that you can later compare notes on the various venues you look at.

ASSESSING THE FACILITIES

Getting there

It may be the intention to take your delegates to a venue off the beaten track so that they are in serene surroundings with little to distract them but the glorious countryside all around. On the other hand, you may be expecting them to travel into a city from various regions of the country and back again on the same day, in which case ease of locating the venue will be of great importance. Consider the following factors:

1. How easy did you find it to locate the venue on your first visit?

2. Is the venue reasonably close to the motorway network or main-line railway station?

3. Will your delegates be driving into a city centre during rush-hour and if so, will the venue still be easy to find?

Assessing the car parking facilities

- Does the facility have adequate car parking? If not, where is the nearest public car park?

- Is there a car park charge?

- Does the hotel have a discount arrangement with the nearest public car park?

- Does the car park appear to be safe, i.e. is it manned, is it in an area where cars are likely to be vulnerable to trouble-makers?

Assessing the suitability of the conference registration area

Ask where the registration desk is usually situated at that particular venue. If the area is not clearly visible to delegates entering the venue, make a note of the fact that adequate signs will be required to point them in the right direction. Ensure that you will have room enough for yourself, staff who may be assisting you, and your delegate packs.

VENUE CHECKLIST

Name of venue

Ease of locating venue

Car parking

Conference room
- style
- capacity
- ceiling height

Toilets
- number of cubicles for ladies
- disabled facilities

Lighting
- blackout facilities
- spotlights
- lectern lights
- location of control panel

Chairs

Obstructions

Exhibition space
- number and location of electricity sockets
- number and location of telephone points
- location in relation to conference

Audio visual equipment
- what does the hotel own?
- how much is included in the costs?
- what is the cost of hiring items from the venue?
- what condition is it in?

Accommodation
- what is the capacity?
- condition of rooms
- facilities provided in rooms, e.g. hairdryers, TV, trouser press, skirt hangers

Catering
- selection of sample menus
- what is included in cost?
- how much do additional teas/coffees, etc cost?
- will lunch be taken standing up or sitting down?

Cloakroom facilities

Pay phone

Charges
- day delegate rate
- 24-hr rate
- room hire rate (if applicable)
- deposit required
- will venue negotiate?

Fig. 2. Venue checklist.

Assessing the rooms

When considering the suitability of any room, be it a large conference room or a small syndicate room, ensure there is adequate space to be able to accommodate the seating plan you are intending using. The most common types are:

- theatre
- classroom
- boardroom
- U-shaped.

These are illustrated in Figure 3. Ask the advice of the hotel or venue staff, who will be very familiar with each style and what works best in their particular rooms.

Working out your needs

How many rooms are you going to require? This will depend on your programme for the event. You may require just one room set in theatre style, or you may be planning to have the delegates split up

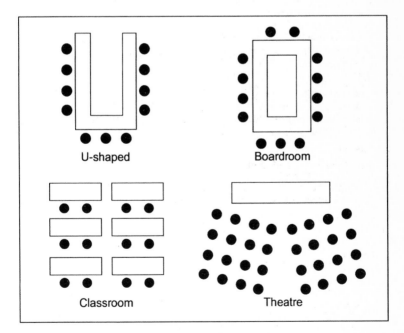

Fig. 3. Seating plans and room styles.

into smaller groups for workshops or smaller meetings. If this is the case you will need to have rooms available which are adequate in size, location and content.

In an ideal world the smaller rooms (or syndicate rooms as they are often called) would be located on the same floor and as close as possible to the main conference room. However, this is often not the case and delegates may have to walk or go by a lift to other floors within the building. If this is the case, are there adequate stairs and/or lifts to be able to cope with the number of people you are expecting? Is there disabled/wheelchair access?

These considerations are important not only in terms of delegate care but to allow you to keep to the schedule. Make a note that adequate signs will be required to ensure delegates don't get lost en route.

Other room considerations

- Be aware that the rooms take time to be set up by the venue staff. Do not expect to be able to run a 500-delegate conference during the day and then follow it by a formal dinner for 500 in the evening in the same room.

- Ask about heating/air conditioning – depending on the time of year, you will certainly need either one or the other.

- Is there a separate room that can be allocated as a speaker room? This is somewhere for the speakers to have some peace and quiet away from the delegates, to maybe run through their slides to make sure they are in the right order and not upside-down, and to generally collect themselves before their talk.

The seating arrangements

If you are expecting a large number of delegates, check that all the seating will be as seen, and not topped up with 'cheap seats'. Sitting still all day is hard enough for most people, but sitting still on uncomfortable chairs is close to impossible!

- Check whether the seating is cushioned and comfortable or hard and uncomfortable.

The ceiling height

Some conference facilities, particularly those on lower ground floors, have particularly low ceilings and little or no natural daylight. If you are expecting a large number of delegates you will need to assess whether this will feel too claustrophobic and, if you are planning on using audio visual equipment, whether the ceiling will allow the use of a screen suitable for your needs. Conversely, the room may have such a high ceiling that the acoustics are difficult to work with.

Assessing the sound
Consider whether microphones will be required in the room and whether there is a sound system already in place.

Looking at the lighting
The quality of lighting can have a dramatic effect on the event. Ambient lighting is usually favoured, with a spotlight on the speaker. Consider the following:

- When the lights go down to darken the room, is your speaker going to disappear too? Will he/she be able to see his notes? If not, a lectern light will be needed.

- Will the audience be able to see to take notes or refer to other literature?

- Where is the control point for the lights situated? In some very modern facilities the control panel is built into the speaker's lectern so they can control the lighting as they see fit; however, by far the most common is a panel at the back of the room.

If you are going to use audio visual equipment you will need to be able to darken the room to a suitable degree. Most modern facilities are able to accommodate blackout, however some older buildings, such as assembly and state rooms, may have high ornate windows with no blinds or shutters.

The staging
You may wish to have your speakers seated on a staged area, especially if you are expecting a large audience.

- Does the venue have its own staging, either permanently fixed or in movable blocks?

- Is there an extra charge for this or is it included in the cost?

Toilets and cloakroom facilities
No one likes queuing for toilets, especially if they only have 15

minutes in which to get a coffee, stretch their legs and dash to the loo! Adequate bathroom facilities are essential, not only for delegate comfort but to ensure that you will physically be able to keep to your scheduled programme. Queues will be inevitable, but keep them within reason.

- Are there adequate disabled facilities?

Particularly in the winter months you may find that delegates wish to leave overcoats and, maybe, overnight bags etc.

- Is a secure cloakroom facility available, and if so it is it manned and is there a charge for this service?
- It may be that a coat rack will be sufficient placed behind the registration desk; is one available for this?

Fire escapes
Do not take anyone else's word for it, check yourself to see that the fire escapes are clear of clutter and that they do conform to safety requirements.

Storage facilities
Is there safe and secure storage space for your own and exhibitors' boxes, etc?

The exhibition space
If you are running an exhibition alongside your conference, or even just displaying information on behalf of the sponsors, ensure that adequate space is available, ideally in the area that will be used for refreshments and not far away from the main conference room. You need to ensure there is room for the actual stands, space for delegates to wander around freely and safely and to establish any Health and Safety regulations which may be enforced by the venue/local authority.

- Are there plenty of electricity sockets?
- Will the exhibitors need a telephone socket? Can this be billed individually by the venue?
- If displaying posters, will suitable display boards be available and what kind of attachment will you need to provide to secure the posters or other graphics to them?

- Are there chairs, tables and table covers available for exhibitors' use?

Identifying obstructions

Have a good look around the potential conference room and see if there are any obstructions that may create problems if not addressed. The most common are pillars situated in unfortunate places that are sure to block the delegates' view, and low-hung chandeliers that look beautiful but may get in the way of the projection equipment. The problems can usually be resolved, or at least worked around.

Assessing the facilities available for disabled delegates

- If the conference rooms are not on the ground floor, is there a suitable sized lift to take anyone using a wheelchair to the appropriate floor?

- Are the disabled toilets within a reasonable distance?

- If you are expecting delegates who may be hard of hearing, has a deaf-loop system been installed?

Assessing the catering facilities

The venue should be able to provide you with a selection of sample menus to give you an idea of what they can provide, for what cost.

- Take a look at the suggested eating area – if it is a fixed restaurant, is it within a reasonable distance from the conference room?

- Will the delegates be taking lunch with other visitors to the venue?

- Is the restaurant located in an area where the delegates are likely to wander back to the exhibition area to the awaiting stand-holders, or are they more likely to wander off to somewhere more interesting?

- What refreshments are included in the price?

- If only morning coffee, lunch and afternoon tea are provided, how much extra will you be required to pay for coffee on arrival?

- Do you intend for lunch to be taken seated or standing up?

- If seated, will there be room for all of your delegates to eat at one sitting?

- With adequate warning is the venue able to cater for specialised diets, e.g. vegetarians, diabetics, etc?

- Very importantly, do the serving staff look cheerful and are they helpful?

- Is the bar area tidy and well stocked?

The accommodation

If you are intending using a hotel facility or any other facility where accommodation is offered and the delegates will be staying overnight, ensure that you also get to view a selection of bedrooms. Consider the following:

- If in a busy city centre are the windows double-glazed?

- What items are available in the rooms?

- Business delegates like to have access to a telephone and many hotels these days also have modem points in the rooms.

- Are tea and coffee-making facilities in the rooms?

- Is a trouser press/iron/hairdryer/skirt hanger provided?

If the venue you are contemplating using does not offer accommodation, the local tourist bureau will be able to help you locate somewhere suitably close to the venue and within your budget. Whilst visiting the venue itself, take time to look at the choice of accommodation available.

ESTABLISHING WHAT IS INCLUDED

Venues vary enormously as to what is included in the price. Traditional hotel and conference centre venues tend to offer both a **day delegate** rate (sometimes called an 8-hour rate), which could include morning coffee, lunch, afternoon tea and use of the conference room. Venues such as hotels that offer accommodation may be able to offer you a **24-hour delegate** rate which usually includes dinner, bed and breakfast as well as the morning coffee, lunch, afternoon tea and use of the conference room. There is normally room for at least some negotiation on both day and 24-hour delegate rates.

Ensuring equipment availability

You will need to ascertain whether the price also includes the hire of the lecterns, microphones, spotlights, screens and staging. If not, find out exactly what items are available, what condition they are in, and how much they will cost to hire. If you are going to use an audio visual technician they may prefer to use their own equipment which is likely to be regularly tested and upgraded, rather than the hotel's own possibly outdated and rather temperamental projector.

CASE STUDIES

Mary is too busy to visit

In her role as social secretary at the Willingby Sports Club, Mary has been asked to organise the first conference run by the club, 'Sporting in the Future' aimed at representatives of other sports clubs across the country. Mary already works part-time and the extra time required to arrange the event is causing her problems. She books a lecture theatre at the university located out of town but doesn't have time to visit. After all, the university staff are used to arranging these things and she isn't. The organising committee manage to persuade some sports companies to exhibit at the event, helping to finance the conference.

The exhibitors arrive on the evening before the conference to set up their stands and are dismayed to find that the exhibition area is in a different building to the conference room. To make the situation worse, the restaurant where lunch and refreshments are to be taken is in yet another building. The conference day dawns and exhibitors are unhappy because few delegates are bothering to visit their stands, the delegates are unhappy because they seem to be spending the day wandering vast distances between sessions, and Mary swears never to run an event again.

Julie lets the train take the strain

Julie has been asked by her PR company boss to arrange a small conference for one of their clients. She contacts a venue-finding service which is able to supply several options and even make a provisional booking at each. Julie has a heavy workload and on receipt of the brochures sent by the venue-finding company is tempted to book the venue of choice over the phone. However, not wishing to take any risks with this valuable client, she decides to travel to the town where the conference is to be held by train, allowing her to work while she travels.

She arrives at the first venue only to find that despite the very well appointed conference room, she is very disappointed by the attitude of the staff, particularly towards other visitors to the hotel who she observes whilst waiting in the reception area. In fact the lady showing her around does not seem particularly interested in this small event. However on visiting the next venue on her shortlist, she finds the staff very pleasant and professional and the conference room far more attractive than the picture she had seen in the brochure.

3

Sourcing Speakers and Setting the Programme

CONDUCTING MARKET RESEARCH

You may be given a brief to produce an event based on a general theme. You will then have to decide on the specific subject areas that are to be included in the programme, and the speakers who are going to present them.

It is important to produce an event in which people are interested enough to invest their time, money and energies to attend. Therefore their opinions matter greatly and some market research can be a worthwhile exercise. To begin your search for subjects a **brainstorming** session with colleagues/superiors can be invaluable. During the session as many different suggestions as possible are called out without discussion and written down for later evaluation. As people bounce ideas off one another, trains of thought can be created and new ideas come to the fore.

DESIGNING A QUESTIONNAIRE

Having brainstormed possible subjects, put together a questionnaire asking potential delegates from in-house or external mailing lists to indicate which of the subjects they would be interested in hearing about. You can also ask them to suggest other subjects and speakers who may not already be listed. From the responses you will be able to put together a programme that you can feel confident is going to be attractive to those you want to attend.

Getting a response

Do not expect a high response rate, typically 5 per cent will respond, so ensure your circular goes to enough potential delegates to make it worthwhile. You can encourage people to respond by making the questionnaire as short as possible, perhaps only one side of A4, and as easy to complete as possible, e.g. using tick boxes and a simple layout. Enclose a stamped addressed envelope or fax-back option and include an incentive such as a discount on the registration fee to those people who return the questionnaire. As with any correspondence that is sent out, be aware of your corporate image and make it as attractive and inviting as possible.

You will need to keep up-to-date on the latest news and views in your particular industry to be able to ensure that the programme is topical.

FINDING SPEAKERS

The importance of good speakers cannot be underestimated. You may have an excellent venue, a large crowd of delegates and have organised it all perfectly, but if the presentations are poor none of it will have mattered. There are certain characteristics to look for in a potential speaker. They should be:

- knowledgeable about the subject
- articulate
- experienced
- well prepared
- able to empathise with, and enthuse, the audience
- respected.

Where to find speakers

Your organisation may have contacts with suitable and willing speakers, however, you may be required to look externally for them.

Call for papers

By notifying appropriate interest groups you may find volunteers who would like to present at the event. The notice can be placed in appropriate journals, sent to university departments, in newsletters, posted on a web site, etc.

The call for papers should include details of the event – date, time, venue – and language of presentation (and whether interpreters will be in attendance) as well as organisers' details. Guidelines should be included as to how to apply. It is usual to ask for a written abstract of a specified number of words which outlines the presentation, as well as a biography of the speaker.

You will find that you will not be short of volunteers. Many companies may find that this opportunity would suit their marketing objectives very well indeed and will be prepared to cover all speaker expenses. If you get more abstracts offered than you need you may be able to hold on to them for future events. (See Figure 4.)

Other events
By attending other similar/competing events, you will be able to identify for yourself which speakers perform well and which don't. Consider how they are received by the audience and in any press reports after the event. Like celebrities, it is possible for speakers to be over-exposed. Popular and prolific speakers are fine so long as their material remains fresh and they do not become complacent. You may also need to book popular speakers some months in advance to ensure their availability.

Speaker bureaux
Speaker bureaux are agencies of, sometimes professional, speakers. A good bureau can be an enormous help in finding the right speaker for your event, but obviously at a price. Some agencies specialise in particular fields and their staff are knowledgeable about the subject matter. Look for a member of the IGAB – International Group of Agencies and Bureaux – so that you can be sure the agency abides by a strict code of practice. They can also provide celebrities for after-dinner speeches, opening ceremonies, etc.

Members of Parliament
Government Ministers and other Members of Parliament are frequently asked to talk at conferences, often in the role of keynote speaker at the start of the event. This can be very worthwhile, particularly in terms of media attraction. As their official diaries tend to be booked well in advance you may need much longer notice of the event than with other speakers. The MPs will often stay only for a short while and will be accompanied by their secretary or assistant and possibly other officials. You will be expected to correspond in detail with the Minister's office to make the necessary arrangements, which may include security and other matters.

CORRESPONDING WITH SPEAKERS

Having chosen your speakers, keep them informed and updated on progress as the conference gets closer. Send them a letter thanking

SECURITY FOCUS '99
UK Security Association Announce 'Call for Papers'

In preparation for the 1999 International Security Focus Conference the UK Security Association would be pleased to receive papers for selection at this important event. The conference, in October 1999 at the National Training Centre in Oxfordshire, will consist of a number of individual sessions each comprising three 35-minute presentations focusing on issues that provide information on the latest trends and issues facing the security industry. Depending on the nature of each session, the attendees will consist of end users, specifiers, manufacturers etc from the UK and overseas, as well as industry-related personnel, including representatives from many police forces, government bodies, etc.

Submissions are welcome from the UK and overseas and should take the following form:

▶ In the first instance an abstract of approx. 500 words should be submitted in English by 15th May 1999 for consideration by an industry panel. Early submissions are encouraged.

▶ Although submissions from commercial companies are very much encouraged, the paper should not be regarded as an advertisement for that company. There will be a number of complementary advertising opportunities during the conference but the content of the presentation should not include direct references to a company's products unless used to illustrate a point.

▶ Papers should be accompanied by a brief career biography of the proposed presenter, including experience of presenting.

▶ On acceptance the speaker will be required to send a full copy of their paper up to 10 sides (5 A4 pages) in length as well as on disk or via email.

▶ For any queries regarding this 'call for papers', please contact Polly Marston at the UK Security Association events office on 01200 789123.

Please send submissions to: Polly Marston, UK Security Association.....

Fig. 4. Call for papers.

them for agreeing to speak, and making clear the terms of the booking. For example, you may or may not be paying a speaker fee or honorarium, travelling expenses, etc. If this is clear from the start there should be no room for misunderstandings later on. (See Figure 5.)

Mr David Church
Area Training Dept
Dental Association of Great Britain
1 Allsorts Gardens
London
SW5

29th October 1999

Dear David,

Ref: Dental Technicians Conference, March 1999

Further to our conversation this morning, I would like to formally invite you to present a paper at the Dental Technicians Conference to be held at the Amblay Manor Hotel and Conference Centre, Wychbold on 15th March 1999.

The conference is an annual event, this year consisting of six papers of 40 minutes duration each. At the end of the conference there will be a question and answer session to the panel of four speakers. This year's chosen theme is **Training and Careers in the Dental Industry** and I know that you are well placed to speak on the subject of **Training into the New Millennium**.

I would like to confirm that we shall be able to pay you a speaker honorarium of £100 plus travelling expenses at 35p per mile or standard class rail fare.

I will forward a speaker information pack to you in the next week which will contain further details of the event. In the meantime if you have any queries please do not hesitate to contact me.

Yours sincerely,

Fig. 5. Invitation to speaker.

Speaker rehearsals

In an ideal world all of the conference speakers would attend a rehearsal in advance of the event to ensure that their presentation skills are satisfactory, that their papers do not overlap in terms of content, that their presentations fill the time schedule correctly and that they are familiar with the venue and audio visual facilities. In reality the first time you meet the speakers will be on the day of the event, half an hour before the start of the presentation. Speakers are often very busy people and, particularly if not being paid for the exercise, may not be inclined to find extra time to travel to the venue or other location to rehearse – in which case, alternatives need to be sought.

Presentation skills

If the speaker is an unknown quantity and you are in any doubt as to the quality of the presentation skills of the speaker, you could travel to meet them and have them do a short presentation for you. Alternatively video footage or anecdotal evidence from experienced and known conference delegates/organisers may help to allay your fears.

Time allocation

Ask the speakers to time themselves rehearsing their presentation and be clear as to whether their time allocation includes questions from the audience, or whether that will be in addition.

Overlap

Overlap can be minimised by providing very clear briefs and issuing a copy of each of the abstracts (or scripts) to each of the speakers, particularly those who are speaking on a similar subject. This, of course, is subject to you being supplied with the abstracts; when requesting them in the speaker pack emphasis should be put on the fact that it really is essential, and will be required at least two weeks (if not longer) in advance of the event. This will allow time for rewriting if necessary. Provide contact details for fellow speakers so that they can discuss presentations if required.

Overseas speakers

You may have an increased chance of speakers arriving for rehearsals if they have flown in from overseas, particularly if they have had a long-haul flight. You should allow for jet-lag when making the flight arrangements and give them adequate time to re-orientate themselves.

Set-up day
It may be possible to set up your conference on the day prior to the event. This will probably result in an additional charge by the venue but this is normally at a reduced rate and is very worthwhile in terms of peace of mind. A good night's sleep is more likely to be had if you have already tested the audio visual equipment, erected the signs, prepared the registration area and set up display stands etc.

Speaker information packs
A pack of information pertinent to the speaker and chairperson will be useful, and could include the following:

Background information on your organisation
They may be unfamiliar with the aims and objectives of your organisation and this will help them to understand 'where you are coming from'.

Overview of event
The aims and objectives of the event and a very brief history if it has run before.

Details of presentation required
A clear brief as to the presentation you are asking them to create and deliver, as well as the duration and timing of it.

Details of the event
Date, time, venue.

Summary of the target audience
The speaker will then be able to adapt his/her talk to suit the understanding of those delegates.

Presentation details of other speakers
Subjects to be covered by other speakers in your session, and possibly contact telephone numbers.

Details of session chairperson
Including contact details if appropriate.

Written requirements
What is required from them in terms of a biography, abstract etc, and when. It is important that you receive this information well in

advance of the event in order for you to be able to distribute it to the chairperson, publish details in the programme etc. Set a date according to your schedule and then move it forward by a week to allow for late responses.

Audio visual requirements form
It is vital to establish what is required well in advance of the event. Emphasise that they should not presume equipment will be available if they have not informed you of its need.

Clear directions/map
Easy to read and accurate.

Details of what to do on arrival
Make it as easy as possible for speakers on the day of the event by giving them details of where to go and what to do on arrival.

Details of lunch/hotel accommodation
Include a note for speakers to inform you if any special dietary requirements are necessary, e.g. vegetarians, allergies, etc.

Include directions to the hotel if different to the venue and make it clear what is being provided, such as 'We will provide bed and breakfast in the Highclere Hotel. Please note that you will be responsible for any other expenses in relation to your stay.'

Parking pass
If applicable.

Useful hints and tips
A few guidelines on how to make the most of their presentation. Even experienced speakers could do with reminding sometimes. See Figure 6.

Details of sponsors
If appropriate.

How and when to claim expenses
If applicable.

Contact details for queries
Details of how and when speakers can reach you, including on-site.

SUGGESTIONS FOR SPEAKERS

- Keep text to a minimum on visual aids.

- Do not blatantly plug your company during your talk. This can have the negative effect of alienating the audience. Your very presence and the high quality of your talk will be an excellent advertisement for your company

- Make eye contact with the audience as often as possible.

- Do not read from a script, use prompt cards instead.

- Rehearse your presentation and ensure it is designed to fit the time allocated. It would be a great shame if the chairperson informed you that you have only two minutes left when you haven't yet reached the main crux of the presentation.

- Ensure you arrive in plenty of time to prepare your visual aids and to generally orientate yourself before your talk.

- Detailed advice for both novice and professional speakers can be found in *Mastering Public Speaking* (How To Books)

Fig. 6. Speaker hints and tips.

A feedback form
Opinion as to the success of the event is important from the speaker's point of view as well as the delegates, so give them an opportunity to be constructively critical.

A checklist for speakers
So that they can easily see when they need to return the various forms, and check themselves to see if they have done so.

UNDERSTANDING THE ROLE OF THE CHAIRPERSON

The **chairperson**'s (or moderator's) role is principally to introduce each speaker to the audience, to ensure they do not overrun their alloted time and to provide the link between each talk. They could also summarise at the end of each talk and field questions from the audience to the speaker or panel of speakers. The chairperson also reads out housekeeping notices such as evacuation details in case of an emergency, order of presentation if changed from the published programme and messages from the organisers. An experienced chairperson who can 'work' an audience is worth his/her weight in gold. Often the job will go to an official from a major sponsor or someone from the organising committee.

CASE STUDIES

Maxine arranges a 'call for papers'

The Equine Behaviour Study Group is organising a conference and Maxine, the Honorary Secretary of the Group, has to find 20 potential presentations of which ten will be chosen by the Study Group Committee.

Maxine draws up a press release announcing the call for papers which is distributed to veterinary journals and veterinary schools in the UK and overseas, as well as to members and associates of the Study Group and past delegates. It is also posted on the Study Group's web site and emailed to the Study Group's electronic mailing list. The resulting abstracts are reviewed and 20 are short-listed. The most worthy ten are presented at the conference and the remaining ten are presented as poster displays during the conference.

Stuart needs a celebrity to add sparkle and generate media interest

Stuart works for a sports injury charity that is launching a campaign to raise money to send disabled sportsmen and women to compete overseas. To complement the launch the charity decides to run a conference to highlight the benefits to disabled people in competing in the worldwide arena. Stuart already has a number of potential speakers linked up through personal and professional contacts, but would like a sporting celebrity to open the conference and deliver the keynote speech. Stuart contacts a speaker bureau which takes details of his specific requirements and makes suggestions with regard to particular speakers who are registered with them. After checking availability and cost they then send him a written proposal and contract.

EXERCISE

Can you think of an example of a conference where you have witnessed a poor presentation? Analyse what it was that made it so poor. Think in terms of the demeanour of the speaker, the delivery of the presentation and consider the rest of the audience's reaction.

4

The Conference Brochure

DESIGNING THE BROCHURE

The brochure is the sales document of the conference. It should appeal to those potential delegates you have identified, set the tone for the event and provide standard information.

Ask yourself a few questions before you start:

- Who is the conference aimed at?

- What information does the brochure need to contain?

- What feedback will you need?

- Are there certain commitments you have made to the sponsors regarding the inclusion and positioning of their logos?

- How will the brochures be circulated?

- How do other organisations design their conference brochures?

Who is it aimed at?
Be sure of who you are targeting. Use language the recipients will be familiar with and avoid the use of unnecessary or irrelevant jargon.

What information should it contain/what feedback will you require?
The brochure will need to contain all necessary information for the delegate, as well as the return booking form containing the information that you will require to process the booking.

Information out	*Information in*
title of conference	name of delegate
description	company
location	position
date	mailing address
time	postcode
speakers	phone number
subjects	fax number
purchase order number	email address

price and method of payment
what's included in price
credit card details if applicable
how to book
closing date for applications
sponsors' details
VAT number
payment method for overseas
    delegates
phone number for enquiries
cancellation policy.

invoice address if different
person to be invoiced
demographics – to be completed
sessions of choice
special dietary requirements.

USEFUL TIPS

Also remember to:

- Leave lots of white space – don't make it look too crowded or over complicated.

- Make it easy to read and understand.

- Edit, re-edit and edit again.

- Make it attractive to look at.

- Make it look professional even if on a tight budget – remember it is your first contact with the delegate and it must impress.

- Make it as simple as possible.

- Even for non-paying events, it is useful to have a form returned so that you can establish how many delegates you will need to cater for.

- Ensure essential information that needs to be retained by the delegates is not placed on the reverse side of the registration form. Further details can be found in Appendix 4.

Choosing who designs it

These days many people are conversant with desktop publishing and are capable of designing their own brochures, a task simplified by dedicated software such as Microsoft Publisher. Ideas can be 'borrowed' from other brochures. Keep a file of any you come across so that you can decide for yourself what works and what doesn't. Alternatively you may consider using a design agency. You will find design agencies listed in local telephone directories, or your local printer may offer this service themselves or may be able to put you in contact with a suitable agency. Obtain several quotes before placing your business as prices will vary considerably. When briefing the agency, ensure your wishes are clear and proof-read the final copy before printing.

Further details of how to create clear and effective documents with a DTP program can be found in *Designing for Desktop Publishing* (How To Books).

PRINTING THE BROCHURE

The look and the feel of the conference brochure will make a big statement about the conference. A shabbily put together document with spelling mistakes and poor grammar will not suggest that the conference will be a well managed, well produced event that your delegates should spend their time and money attending. Conversely, a well designed, glossy brochure that is clear and concise will put the potential delegate in a positive frame of mind.

Choosing the paper

Choose the paper carefully. If you are working on a tight budget you may not be able to afford glossy paper, but you could make good use of colour. Pastel shades are easy on the eye and will also fax clearly, conversely a deep colour will often be illegible after faxing.

Use at least 100gsm paper – it needs to be resilient and withstand being photocopied, filed, mailed and returned. If you are incorporating a reply-paid coupon then the Post Office requires the thickness to be no less that 235 microns and A6 minimum in size.

Proof-read time and time again. And when you are sure everything is correct, do it again. Also ask at least one other person to go over it as you may find that you have become 'blind' to mistakes if you have been working on the document for too long.

Costing the printing

As with design agencies, the cost of printing will vary from company to company and from paper type to paper type, so obtain a selection of quotes. Generally the first print run will include the preparation of the plates used in the printing process, and the cost difference per thousand after that will not be huge. It will be helpful to let the printer know in advance when to expect the camera ready copy, and the date by which the finished documents will be needed. This will enable the printer to build it into the print schedule. If possible give printers a deadline which is earlier than necessary to allow for unseen circumstances. Also bear in mind that print runs required at short notice will often cost more. An absolute minimum of one week will be required.

DISTRIBUTING THE BROCHURE

Having given much thought to the content and design of the brochure, you now need to get it in front of your potential delegates. Who they are will determine how you reach them.

Mailing options
- in-house mailing lists

- membership lists

- previous delegates

- purchasing lists from mailing companies

- magazine inserts

- 'piggy back' mailings with companies you may have connections with who are targeting similar individuals

- lists obtained from publications, directories, registers and the local Chamber of Commerce.

If you can send the brochure to a named individual rather than 'Marketing Manager, XYZ Products Ltd' for example, it will be much more likely to reach them.

Whether using in-house or bought-in mailing lists, ensure they are 'clean', i.e. names are not duplicated. As well as being uneconomical, in our world of constant unsolicited junk mail people have low tolerance thresholds.

Electronic distribution
If your organisation has a web site, put the programme and booking details on it.

Postage
If doing a very large mailing, professional mailing houses will fill the envelopes, frank and dispatch them for a fee, and a reduction can

sometimes be gained in the mailing cost. Ask your Post Office about Mailsort and Press Stream which are discount services for mailings of over 4,000 items.

EXERCISES

1. Experiment with what you can achieve on your own PC. Does the finished product look professional?

2. Find out what resources are available within your local public library for making up your own mailing lists.

5

Working to a Schedule

SCHEDULING THE EVENT

Twelve weeks can normally be considered an adequate lead-time for events. This allows satisfactory time for preparation, and for press releases to be received and published in the relevant monthly journals. Prior to the 12-week countdown to the event you will have:

- set the budget
- researched and booked the venue
- decided on the content of your programme and copy for the brochure
- booked the speakers
- and be ready to mail out the printed programmes.

When to send the brochure
Events, organisations and budgets will combine to dictate what is and what is not possible. Presuming the initial mailshot is sent 12 weeks in advance of the event it could be followed by a written or telephone reminder to those who have not yet booked at eight weeks, and then again four weeks out.

Although requiring longer notice of events, there is a tendency for delegates to book their place as late as possible, especially if purchase orders have to be passed through accounting departments. Although to be expected, this can be frustrating for the organiser who needs to be able to anticipate delegate attendance numbers as early as possible. It can be useful to offer an 'early bird' price to encourage early bookings. The resulting increase in early registrations will provide an indication of how the event is being received by potential delegates. This can be useful to help you plan and implement your promotional activity.

Finding other targets
By analysing delegate details as they book you can target other

potential delegates. For instance, if you find that the conference is attracting a large number of people in a particular job function, or in similar demographic groups, you could direct-mail other people in similar positions.

CREATING A PLAN

Time is a valuable resource of which few of us seem to have enough. Once time has passed it cannot be replaced, so use it wisely. Whether it is your free time or your work time it is difficult to place an exact figure on the cost of you performing a given task.

> A well structured approach to the task of organising your conference is essential and will bring many benefits.

Benefits of using a time plan
- You will be able to identify tasks and allocate staff/resources/ your own time as required to deal with them.

- You will be able to organise your normal work-load around the event and the organisation.

- By their very nature some tasks must be done at the last minute, e.g. preparation of badges and stuffing delegate packs. Others need to be carried out some time in advance, such as finding sponsors and distributing programmes. A visual plan will help you to put the pieces together in the correct order and fill any gaps with tasks that, within reason, have no time requirements, like choosing menus. See Figures 7 and 8, which indicate key elements that must be addressed and can be used as a basis for your own plan.

SCHEDULING THE PROGRAMME

Your brief will dictate the duration of the event – a day, evening or two days perhaps. The programme has to fill that space adequately, ensuring delegates have time to absorb what they're hearing, but not get bored. Remember that we all have relatively short concentration spans, so shorter bursts of information interspersed with lighter input are most likely to be retained.

Wk bg.					
Before or during Wk 12	**Wk 11**	**Wk 10**	**Wk 9**	**Wk 8**	**Wk 7**
Design/print/ distribute programme			Receive sponsors' payments	Establish exhibitor requirements	
Confirm venue/ speakers/ sponsors (& invoice sponsors)	Send speaker packs		AV form returns start		AV forms returned
Block-book hotel	Set up registration system		Order sponsored items, e.g. bags		
Book/confirm contractors		Send sponsor & exhibitor info. packs			
Advance press notice & monthly mags	Design/seek approval of layout of sponsored items		Press release1		

Wk 6	**Wk 5**	**Wk 4**	**Wk 3**	**Wk 2**	**Event Week**
Confirm menus	Print bags	Photocopy speaker papers etc	Take delivery of delegate pack inserts	Closing date for applications	Everything not done between wk 12 & now!
Confirm AV requirements to contractor	Hotel room allocation	Revisit venue & conduct risk assessment	Take delivery of sponsored items, e.g. pens etc.	Prepare delegate packs	
	Press release 2		Provide approx. catering nos.	Press release 3	
	Invoice sponsors		Circulate rehearsal schedule	Confirm final numbers to venue	
	Print catalogue or programme			Confirm final rooming list	

Post event: analyse evaluation forms, finalise budget and debrief. Ongoing throughout 12-week countdown: handle registration/enquiries.

Fig. 7. Time plan illustration (i).

This planner is less detailed and monitors only key tasks. It could be used in conjunction with a more detailed planner.

Task	Target Date	Completion Date	Actioned by
Identify brief			
Budget projection			
Budget actual			
Venue visits			
Venue confirmation			
Speaker programme confirmed			
Brochure design/print			
Brochures mailed			
PR activity Pre-event 1, 2 & 3 Post-event			
Accommodation booked			
Delegate pack items received & packed			
AV requirements confirmed			
De-brief			

Fig. 8. Time plan illustration (ii).

Timing it right

The right time to start
Consider how the majority of delegates are likely to travel to the venue. By car? By train? By tube? Avoiding the necessity for travel in peak times if at all possible will help ensure delegates arrive in a good frame of mind.

Refreshment breaks
Ensure adequate time is built into the programme for the number of anticipated delegates to get themselves a drink and go to the toilet during the refreshment breaks. Similarly at lunchtime the delegates

A Closer Look at Ethology

(Including half-day workshops on cats, horses and rabbits)

09.30 – 10.00	Registration
10.00 – 10.05	Welcome
	David Appleby Dip CABC
10.05 – 10.50	Evolutionary constraints on species specific behaviour in the cat
	John Bradshaw PhD
10.50 – 12.05	Problem horses? Problem owners? Understanding equine behavioural strategies
	Cecilia Lindberg BA, MA, PhD
12.05 – 12.50	Behaviour modification – working with natural behaviours
	Emma Magnus BSc(Hons) MSc
12.50 – 14.00	Buffet lunch
14.00 – 15.15	Workshops

1: Understanding and reducing stress in cats – a practical approach
Sarah Heath BVSc MRCVS and Sandra McCune VN BA(Mod) PhD

2: The Natural Horse
Neil Davidson BSc(Hons) and Natalie Waran PhD

3: Benjamin Bunny or Roger Rabbit? Rabbit behaviour problems – prevention and modification.
Anne McBride BSc, PhD, Cert Cons, FRSA and Christine Huggett BSc(Hons) PhD.

15.15 – 15.45	Coffee
15.45 – 16.30	Workshops as above
16.30	Depart

Fig. 9. Conference programme.

will need to get to the lunch room, consume their lunch, network, stretch their legs and get some fresh air, and go to the toilet. The number and location of toilets available at the venue of your choice, the location of the lunch room, the presence of exhibitors and the number of delegates will have a direct bearing on these timings.

Location of conference rooms

If the conference is spread throughout a number of rooms, ensure that enough time is built into the programme for the delegates to be able to move from one to another. This is particularly important if the rooms are on different floors. It is very distracting and most unfair to speakers to have delegates wandering into their presentations late. Consider how the delegates will move from one room to another. Do they need to use a lift? If so, how many lifts are there? Where are they situated? How many 'lift-loads' of delegates are going to be moving? Do not base this judgement on the time it takes you and the venue co-ordinator to walk the same route during your recce. Delegates will walk slower, will probably be chatting and not necessarily paying attention to signs, or they may get distracted by something more interesting along the way. Even if the rooms are located on the same floor and close together still expect some delay. Delegates will use the opportunity to nip to the toilets, make phone calls and to get some fresh air.

The graveyard slot

After lunch everyone undergoes a lull whilst our bodies are busy digesting food. The resulting dip in energy levels means that whilst the speaker is getting high on nerve-induced adrenalin the delegates are resisting the urge (hopefully) to fall asleep, hence the term 'graveyard slot'. To help keep everyone on their toes, make sure the room is not too warm and schedule a lively and entertaining speaker with a particularly interesting subject.

Consecutive days

If running at two-day event, delegates may not need to register on the second day. It is wise not to start too early in the morning if the schedule allows, as you may find delegates wander in late. Alternatively put a very interesting paper that no one wants to miss on first.

The date of your event may be dictated to you, giving you no control over it. Alternatively you may have some freedom to decide on the best date.

Weekend or weekday?
Weekend rates are usually substantially cheaper, however choosing a weekend may not be suitable for a business event.

Holiday time or competing events?
Consider the time of year. Are there any other major events being held which would draw your delegates away? Is it a peak holiday time? Too soon before/after Christmas? This can be of particular importance if delegates will be paying their own fees and expenses rather than companies.

CASE STUDIES

Michael's conference goes down the pan
Michael is running his first event and is desperate to ensure that it all goes to plan. In his haste to print the brochures ready for dispatch, his failure to build into the programme a morning coffee break has gone unnoticed. When the error is discovered, Michael decides to amend the programme by reducing the three morning speakers' question and answer sessions by five minutes, thus allowing time for a 15-minute coffee break.

Unfortunately the 180 delegates have only just finished being served their tea when the call is made for delegates to return to the hall. As delegates wander off to find toilets instead of heading straight back to the conference hall, a further 15 minutes has passed and the day is now running late. The speaker is becoming agitated by the constant disturbance of returning delegates and there is a danger of upsetting the exhibitors by announcing a shorter lunch break (therefore shorter time to view the stands) to make up lost time.

Rachel just cannot get a response
Rachel has been asked to arrange a conference at short notice, and to be successful in terms of delegate numbers it is essential that the conference is brought to the attention of as many potential delegates as possible. Her industry is served by several glossy magazines that are taken and keenly read by most individuals involved in the industry. Unfortunately the deadline for all of the journals has long since passed and the resulting intensified direct mail campaign proves costly.

Attendance at the event itself is, not surprisingly, low and Rachel receives many letters after the event, of which this one is typical:

Dear Rachel Pordy
Thank you for sending details of the Dried Flower Association conference entitled 'Dried Flowers – a professional opportunity?' Unfortunately I was unable to attend due to the late notice but would be grateful if you could send me details of any conference papers etc that may be available. I would also request that my contact details are added to your mailing list in the hope of receiving earlier notification.

Yours...

EXERCISE

Consider the nature of your organisation. Research and list all the events (conferences, exhibitions, etc) which take place within it that could be inviting to your potential delegates. Are there any noticeable gaps in the calendar which would be suitable for your conference?

6

Setting up a Registration System

USING COMPUTERISED REGISTRATION SYSTEMS

There are an increasing number of software packages available to conference organisers that can streamline the whole registration process. By entering the delegate details just once you can automatically produce:

- a personalised letter of confirmation
- a badge
- an invoice
- and allocate workshops, hotel bookings, etc.

Modules can be incorporated to plan and track accommodation, catering, partner programmes, excursions, budgets, etc and may also include a register of venues. Each of the growing number of software packages have different benefits and considerations so it is worth seeing a demonstration of each, and if possible talking to current users of the systems. Most can be networked so that a number of people can access and use the system. Some can be purchased in modules allowing you to pay for only those modules that will be of use to you. As is standard with most computer software packages, technical support is available for registered users.

Assessing costs
Always look carefully at the cost and terms of the support offered, which although probably essential can, in some cases, be quite prohibitive. However, the time that these software packages can save in administration and reporting can be very substantial.

Modifying your existing software
If you are organising your first conference for a society or association you may well not have the luxury of a dedicated software program. In this case one alternative is to have your own

program written by a computer programmer. It can be designed to suit your exact requirements and hardware but will still incur possibly high costs in programmers' fees. If considering your own custom-made program remember that technical support may still be needed on an on-going basis, and check that the programmer will be able to provide this.

OTHER REGISTRATION OPTIONS

Data companies
Some organisations choose to delegate the registration process to a specialist registration company. These companies are experienced in handling registrations for all kinds of conferences and exhibitions, and can provide other associated services such as invoicing, credit control, badging, mailings, etc. The companies can provide staff and the equipment for computerised on-site registration as well as handling pre-event registrations. It is worth discussing your requirements with one or two registration companies to establish exactly what they can do for you, and at what cost.

What they offer
What can they offer that you cannot, or most likely do not have time to do yourself? The cost of professional registration services may prove prohibitive for the smaller conference but with larger events are worth giving some consideration to. As with all event professionals, do not think of the cost alone. Consider the other, less tangible, benefits of having experienced personnel with a computerised and efficient system in the front line.

Dealing with registration in-house
You may decide to handle the bookings and enquiries yourself, or at least keep it in-house. This need not be the daunting task it may appear, so long as a system is put into place to ensure that it is as automated as possible. Decide on your system before the first bookings arrive.

SETTING UP YOUR OWN IN-HOUSE MANUAL SYSTEM

All delegates registering to attend the event, whether fee-paying or otherwise, will require a confirmation that their booking has been received and they are expected to attend. The confirmation document can include a number of items such as directions, instructions for when they arrive, reminder of the registration time, etc. Ensure the letter, in keeping with the brochure and any other literature issued, is attractive, unambiguous and follows the house-style if appropriate.

What to include in the information pack

Directions
The venue should be able to provide you with a map to issue to all attendees. Make sure that it is up-to-date. It is not uncommon for new roundabouts and traffic systems to be put in place whilst the venue merrily carries on issuing the same map, causing unnecessary grief to the delegates in the process.

There are companies who will provide maps of any given area customised to your own specification. These look very attractive and can incorporate your own logos. (Perhaps yet another sponsorship opportunity?)

Invoice/receipt
You will have already established whether or not payment is to be made at the time of booking or whether individuals can be invoiced. This is a decision that should be made in conjunction with the organisation's accounting department or honorary treasurer. Similarly credit card payments will need to be processed according to the organisation's normal practice. The registration process can get very complicated if the payments have to be separated and sent to the accounts department for processing, and the protracted process can also increase the room for error and mislaid documents. You will have to discuss the implications of this with appropriate management and find a system that will work for you all.

Confirmation details
The letter of confirmation should be, as usual, within the company/ organisation's corporate image, and should be welcoming and clear. Instructions should be precise and unambiguous. Remind delegates of the registration time and whether coffee will be available to them on arrival. (See Figure 10.)

Badges
Some organisers dispatch badges with the letter of confirmation to save time and prevent unnecessary queuing during the registration

Please reply to:
Pauline Appleby, Conference Manager
Interface, Upper Street, Defford, Worcs
WR8 9AB. Tel: 01386 750534
Mobile: 0385 567487 Fax: 01386 750743
Email: pauline@petbcent.demon.co.uk

Dear Mr Trevor Morgan

Virtual World Conference – Wednesday 12th June 200X

Thank you for registering to attend the Virtual World Conference at the Multi Media Centre, University of Woodlow. I have pleasure in enclosing your receipt and a map/directions for your convenience. The University lies to the west of the Uplands–Barlow section of the A985 (Barlow Road) and to the south-west of the A85 (Markets Road), about 6 miles south of Worcester, and $1^1/4$ miles north of Malvern. The Multi Media Centre is accessed from the **Central Campus entrance.**

Travel & useful numbers
By train: Nearest station – Malvern (hourly service from London Paddington – journey time 2 hrs). Full timetable details can be obtained by calling 0345 484950.
National Express coaches: 0990 808080.
By road: Approx, journey time from London 2 hrs, Oxford 1 hr. Birmingham 40 mins.
By air: Birmingham International Airport 0121 767 5511.
Taxi: Jim's Taxis 01684 555555.

We look forward to welcoming you for coffee and registration between 8am and 9.15am on Wednesday 12th June.

If you have any queries regarding your booking please do not hesitate to contact me on 01386 750534.

With kind regards,
Yours sincerely

Pauline Appleby
Conference Manager

Enc: Map/VAT Invoice

Fig. 10. Delegate confirmation letter.

period. If this is the case they should be instructed to bring the badge with them to gain entry and to collect a badge holder (if used) when they register.

Make a note of all correspondence with delegates so that you know exactly what has been dispatched and when. Should any delegates have any queries you will then be able to immediately check the dispatch details. Keeping a file of the completed and processed booking forms, in alphabetical order to be taken on site, will ensure that you will quickly be able to look up any particular delegate's queries.

Notification of workshop allocation
If workshop places have been designated, relevant details such as time and location could be included in the letter of confirmation.

A list of useful numbers and travel hints
Supply the name and telephone number of a local taxi firm, rail enquiry number, nearest airport, etc. Also indicate the most convenient tube station if the event is in London. By contacting London Transport you may be able to obtain tube maps and other helpful leaflets that you can include in the information pack.

REGISTERING DELEGATES ON-SITE

It is important that the registration system which you decide upon is as simple as possible. Before the arrival of computerised registration systems it was usual for badges to be laid out in alphabetical order on the registration desk. This is derided these days by some professional organisers, but although not terribly sophisticated it is a reliable and effective method of registering delegates. The badges are easy to locate as each individual arrives at the desk, and it is easy to see at a glance who is and who is not in attendance. For security reasons an alternative method is to put the badges in alphabetical order in a long box so that unregistered delegates are unable to 'assume' the identity of someone who is pre-registered. If packs, papers, bags, etc are also to be handed out ensure they are laid out in an obvious order. If space allows you could have separate tables so that delegates can register and collect their badge at one table and then move on to a second table to collect their packs etc. This also encourages delegates to move away from the main area of registration as quickly as possible.

Keep an area free for dealing with late payments and queries, and ensure that you have all the items to hand that you may need, such as receipts, pens and credit card facilities. Remember to book a phone line if an automated credit card facility is to be used.

CASE STUDY

Amy avoids problems with numbers

Amy is running a conference targeted at volunteers who give their time to promote the charity for which she works. Its objective is to instil a professional attitude to their fund-raising, promotion and dealings with the public. The event is complimentary, and a sum of money has been allocated from the education budget to cover all costs. Five hundred volunteers have been notified of the conference, and it is anticipated that approximately 200 will attend. As the event is free of charge, it is feasible for the volunteers to decide very late whether or not they will attend. This could create problems and possible waste of money if the catering numbers cannot be confirmed in advance, and will be embarrassing if more than the anticipated number arrive without adequate seating being available.

To avoid these problems, and to increase a sense of commitment in the volunteers, Amy asks volunteers to complete and return a registration form. On receipt of this she sends the volunteer an acknowledgement which includes a map of how to find the venue and a badge which the volunteer must bring along to gain entry.

Amy is then able to advise the caterers on the number of lunches and other refreshments required and also advises the venue co-ordinator on the number of chairs to be set out.

EXERCISE

Next time you attend an event, observe the registration area. Are there long queues? Do the staff appear informed, relaxed and welcoming? Consider what could be done differently.

7

Planning Budgets and Sponsorship

SETTING BUDGETS

Before even starting to think about venues, location, speakers, etc the budget must be established. The budget is a quantitative goal which states the financial confines in which you are working. It is the target against which costings (the actual price you will be paying) will be measured. The budget may be given to you as part of your brief, or it may be up to you to prepare your own budget and to justify the costs to your superiors. If a substantial amount of the costs are to be met by sponsorship, you will need to prepare a plan as to how you are going to achieve it. All of this needs to take place before you start your event countdown.

Looking at the costs

Although the budget should be set at the start of the project it can be altered and monitored as you proceed. The combined costs must fall within your budget figures.

Fixed costs

Fixed costs are those costs that will be encountered irrespective of the number of delegates who may attend. For example:

- brochure printing
- brochure design
- organisation fees
- speaker fees
- travel
- accommodation
- room hire
- press and publicity
- advertising
- mailing house
- signs.

NW Regional Conference – Budget

		Income	Expenditure	Total	
Fixed costs					
	Venue hire		175.00		
	Print brochure		750.00		
	Speaker fees		350.00		
	Mailing		300.00		
	Advertising/PR		250.00		
	AV hire		300.00	2125.00	
Variable costs					
	Buffet/refreshments £15 x 150		2250.00		
				4375.00	
	Exhibitors @ £250.00				
	5	1250	Profit	(3125.00)	
	10	2500		(1875.00)	
	15	3750		(625.00)	

This example budget is for a non-profit making conference and assumes that the design of brochure and supply of staff has been handled in-house. This could also be itemised if necessary to identify the true cost of the event. Bracketed figures indicate negative amounts.

Fig. 11. Example budget – projected.

NW Regional Conference – Budget

		Income	Expenditure	Total	Actual	Actual total
Fixed costs						
	Venue hire		175.00		175.00	
	Print brochure		750.00		725.00	
	Speaker fees		350.00		350.00	
	Mailing		300.00		287.00	
	Advertising/PR		250.00		207.00	
	AV hire		300.00	2125.00	320.00	2064.00
Variable costs						
	Buffet/ refreshments £15 x 150		2250.00		2070.00	
				4375.00		4134.00
	Exhibitors @ £250.00					
	5	1250	Profit	(3125.00)		
	10	2500		(1875.00)	1875.00	(2259.00)
	15		3750	(625.00)		

The actual figures indicate that the conference has cost £2259.00 to produce.

Fig. 12. Example budget – actual.

Variable costs
Variable costs are those which vary according to the number of delegates who attend, e.g. catering costs.

Income
Income may come from different sources and can also be categorised as **fixed** and **variable**.

Fixed income
Income that is not dependent on the number of delegates. For example:

- sponsorship
- contribution from organisation
- exhibition stands.

Variable income
Income that is not fixed. It may for example vary according to the number of delegates purchasing tickets.

Value Added Tax
Value Added Tax (VAT) will be added to many costs of goods and services supplied and will be added to the ticket price if your organisation is registered for VAT. For the purpose of the budget the VAT should not be included on any of the entries so that a true figure is seen. The exception to this rule is if the organising company or organisation is not VAT registered, in which case they will not charge VAT on the ticket sales and will be unable to reclaim VAT on expenditure so the entire cost will need to be met.

Breaking even
A **break-even point** is the point at which the conference makes enough income to cover the fixed costs. If the conference is income-generating it is important to know what this figure is so that you have a quantifiable goal to aim for. To find the break-even point, see Figure 13. Further details on practical budgeting can be found in *Managing Budgets and Cash Flows* (How To Books).

INSURING AGAINST DISASTERS
The thorny issue of insurance should be addressed and a management

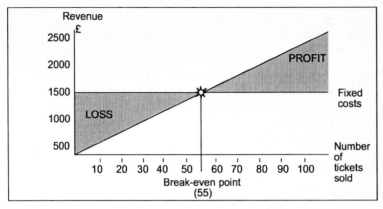

Fig. 13. Finding the break-even point.
We can see that 55 tickets need to be sold to
break even to meet the fixed costs of £1,500.

decision made as to whether or not to take up one of the specialised
insurance policies that are available. No matter how hard we try, some
things really are beyond our control, such as the weather, rail strikes,
terrorist activity, etc. In instances where conferences are drastically
affected by these things, adequate and appropriate insurance can
make the difference between an inconvenience and a financial disaster.
Policies can be taken out to reimburse organisers for a range of
mishaps, including:

- cancellation/abandonment

- non-appearance of speakers

- reduced attendance by delegates

- failure to vacate the venue by the specified time

- legal liabilities

- personal accident and travel.

Checking your cover
Check your organisation's own insurance policy and establish the
situation regarding the venue's insurance policy. The items left
uncovered by either of these are what you now need to look at. There
are several specialist insurance companies who can provide flexible
packages, so discuss your situation and obtain quotes from them.
You may be surprised at how reasonable the premium can be.

CONTROLLING THE CATERING COSTS

Every venue you visit will be able to supply you with an assortment of menus that can be provided in a range of budgets. You may be offered a day delegate rate which includes lunch and refreshments or you may be offered a room hire rate with catering costs separate. This is often the case with civic and more unusual buildings, where the facility is leased to a catering company and all payments relating to catering costs are made directly to them. If offered a day delegate rate check exactly what it includes. How many servings of tea and coffee does it include? It may only be two, in which case you may need to order another serving for registration. Is the lunch price for a finger buffet, fork buffet or a more formal seated meal? How many courses?

Considering drinks

Are soft drinks included in the price? If not, what are the costs? Very often the soft drinks such as mineral water and orange juice are charged per bottle or carton used, so you only pay for what you use. If this is the case it is important to give the caterers a limit so that they notify you when it has been reached. The amount can add up very quickly and work out very costly if you do not control it.

These days delegates tend not to expect wine with their meal as was traditionally the case. Hotels may have their own bar as well as having a temporary bar facility in the conference area. Many organisers opt to let delegates purchase their own drinks at the hotel bar rather than having the temporary one opened. Sober delegates make for much happier delegates and the after-lunch slump is made many times worse if delegates have been drinking alcohol. If wine is to be served it will be charged at premium rates and it can be false economy to provide your own. The corkage charge made by the venue for every bottle opened may result in you paying even more.

Making compromises

Some organisers have the luxury of working with a large budget and minimum restriction on catering and other costs. More common, though, is the organiser with a limited budget who is still required to provide the best of everything.

If you are working to a restricted budget and are finding it difficult to make ends meet there are a few compromises that can be made.

- Question whether you need to serve biscuits with each serving of tea and coffee. If not, this could be a worthwhile saving and is especially practical if a sweet is being included in the lunch.

- A buffet lunch will always be more cost effective than a seated lunch. Select the items carefully, e.g. a wholesome lasagne and jacket potato will be both filling and cost effective.

- Check whether you are to be charged room hire for the use of the lunch room. Often if you are having catering there will be no room hire charge, however this is not always the case and it is an area that may be open to negotiation.

NEGOTIATING RATES

Do not be inhibited about negotiating the room rates. Venues do not come with immovable price tags attached. They will have a rack rate which is the full quoted price, but very often this is the starting price and there is almost always some room for manoeuvre. Start at a price lower than you would expect them to accept so that a compromise will lead you to a more realistic target. Don't forget, if you start high you cannot get lower. Although you will probably be asked directly, avoid telling them exactly what your budget is. Keep it as vague as possible to start with, 'This is being run on a tight budget'; 'We have a reasonable budget but it is likely we will still require some compromise on both our parts'. Appear cool and confident when negotiating. However much you may like this particular venue, remember there are many alternative venues you could use, and the venue co-ordinator will be aware of that.

If you are preparing a series of conferences around the country you may also be able to gain an extra discount by using a hotel chain that will give a discount for multiple bookings.

If you do not feel that you can negotiate well, ask the venue-finding agency to do it on your behalf. They are very experienced at such things and may already have a discount arrangement.

What to look for
The 'package' that will be offered can vary hugely between one venue and the next. All have their advantages and disadvantages and the benefits must be weighed up considering the type of event you are organising. As a rule, purpose-built training centres often have more equipment included in the room hire rate than most hotels. This can include whiteboards, TV and video monitors and other audio visual equipment. Some venues may include an organiser's office, the speaker room, the lectern, staging and tables in their price.

Paying professionals

It is likely that you will need to bring in other event professionals at some point during the preparation for and the running of the event. Printers, audio visual technicians, stage designers and freelance organisers have their own rates and these should be made clear from the start. Establish whether expenses are to be added on to their basic fee and establish payment terms.

Playing safe

Ensure a contingency fund is built into the budget. This will cover unforeseen expenses and will help to ensure that your budget does not get out of control.

ARRANGING SPONSORSHIP

Having decided to seek sponsorship in one form or another from one or more companies, draw up a list of companies and/or organisations that would benefit from reaching the type of delegates that you are hoping to attract yourself.

The benefit to sponsors is the opportunity to directly communicate with potential customers, to raise their company profile whilst meeting their marketing objectives. The benefit to you is that they will be paying for the privilege and so providing some often much needed cash.

Your options are to obtain either full sponsorship from one company, or to break down the various elements that could be sponsored and offer them to a variety of organisations.

Looking at sponsorship opportunities

You are limited only by your imagination when it comes to thinking of items to have sponsored. From biros to baseball caps, from balloons to briefcases, there will be a promotional gift company that will be able to satisfy your needs. There are currently at least two major trade shows dedicated to the incentive and promotional gift market. Take a trip to one of these and you will be able to discuss your requirements in detail with suppliers, and gather ideas and examples from the items on display. You may also be able to take advantage of special show offers giving you a significant discount on your orders.

Carpet Manufacturers Association

Autumn Conference

Item	Benefits	Cost	Confirm choice	Please call to discuss
Delegate bags (linen shoulder bags)	• High visibility • Post-event use • Includes 2 free delegate places	£1,000 200 bags		
Notebooks and pens	• Continued use provides visual reminder	£750 200 A4 notebooks 200 boxed pens		
Delegate pack inserts	• Provides cost-effective marketing opportunity to targeted decision makers	£250 200 A4 flyers required by 20th September		
Programme advertisement – ½ page	• Association with quality event	£150 CRC to be received by 1st September		
Programme advertisement – whole page	• Association with quality event	£200 CRC to be received by 1st September		

All sponsorship opportunities include sponsors' logo on the conference brochure. Prices are exclusive of screen print charge and VAT. Total cost will be confirmed at time of booking.

Name:

Position:

Company:

Address:

Tel:　　　　　　　　Fax:　　　　　　　　Email:

Please return this form to Jim May at the Carpet Manufacturers Association, Carpet House, 73 Brighton Road, Bournemouth. Tel: 01412 334556.

Fig. 14. Sponsorship opportunity form.

Knowing what to charge sponsors

Draw up a list of items you think would be appropriate to your event and work out the cost of those items to be produced, including the screen-print charge and delivery. Then add on a percentage which is the sponsor's contribution to the event. The amount will vary according to your particular circumstances. (When calculating the cost of the screen-printing be aware of the increase in charges if using more than one colour.)

How to contact potential sponsors

Circulate a letter of introduction and a sponsorship form to your list of potential sponsors, making sure it looks professional and attractive. Ensure that it clearly stresses the benefits to the organisation should they decide to take up the opportunity. Be totally honest about the expected number of delegates, mailing, numbers of brochures, etc. Include a date by which forms should be returned, and be sure to enclose a contact name and telephone number for any queries.

Confirming the sponsorship agreement

Having obtained an initial agreement to sponsor the event, send a written sponsorship agreement, making it clear exactly what is included in the package, confirming the cost, and informing them of the date that the invoice will be sent and the terms of payment. This ensures that it is clear from the start that there is no room for misinterpretation. Sponsors should be invoiced before the relevant items are ordered, so that should they have a last minute change of heart you are not left to pick up the bill for 200 delegate bags with their logo printed on them.

Logos are designed at great expense and play an important part in a company's corporate identity. It is essential that designs for your sponsored items are approved by the company.

TAKING CARE OF SPONSORS

Having provided the financial resources to enable you to hold your event it is worth looking after your sponsors. Without them the financial outlay could render the event unviable and, of course, you may wish to approach them again in future years. In terms of physical products – pens, bags, brochures etc – send a set to the sponsor when they have been produced. In the case of brochures

23rd January 199X

Mr A Wilson
Wildlife Magazine
22 York Road
Dover

Dear Mr Wilson

Thank you for agreeing to sponsor the West Midlands Nature Centre's Conference 'A Walk on the Wild Side' to be held on 22nd May.

I would like to confirm that you have chosen the option of sponsored notebooks and pens which will be placed inside the delegate packs. This option also includes two free places at the conference. An invoice for the agreed sum of £750 will follow under separate cover.

Please forward a bromide or tiff file of your company logo, along with any guidelines for its placement. I will send a copy of the notebook design incorporating your logo for your approval as soon as possible.

I am sure that you will find this a worthwhile opportunity and look forward to speaking to you again in due course.

Yours sincerely

Fig. 15. Sponsorship confirmation letter.

that carry their logo, you may find that the sponsor is willing to distribute brochures on your behalf as it can be of mutual benefit.

After the event
After the event send a personalised thank you letter to the sponsor. If the delegate list was to be part of the sponsorship agreement, ensure this is also sent promptly.

Sponsorship ideas
- advertisement in brochure
- dinner

- wine
- cocktail reception
- flowers
- luncheons/bags/documentation
- pens/badges
- notepads
- signs
- conference speaker expenses
- carpet tiles
- banners
- breakfasts.

Further details on seeking sponsorship can be found in *How to Raise Funds and Sponsorship* (How To Books).

EXERCISES

1. A contingency fund of some 5 per cent of the overall budget should be included in the budget. List what could necessitate its use.

2. A list of sponsorship opportunities is included in the chapter. Think of others which would be appropriate to your own organisation, and define why sponsors would be attracted to your event.

8

Assessing the Audio Visual Requirements

Different events and different speakers have specific audio visual requirements. It is important that you establish early on in the planning process what is available in the venue of your choice, what each speaker's requirements are, and the costs involved. Do not take for granted the condition and quality if using in-house equipment. Without a specialist to look after it the equipment may be out-dated, have intermittent faults or be of low quality.

LOOKING AT THE CHOICE OF VISUAL PROJECTION

Traditionally presentations were given with the aid of an **overhead projector (OHP)** or by **slide projection** (35mm). These are still used today, but becoming more popular are computer generated presentations, made using specialist but commonly available software to produce an assortment of visual imagery.

The benefit of a more technical presentation in terms of projection equipment, when used well, is dramatically increased visual stimulation for the delegates. The down side is that the more sophisticated equipment involved, the more room there could be for error, which could, in the worst case scenario, result in a flustered speaker with no visual aids and a room full of bored and restless delegates.

Overhead projector (OHP)

Clear acetate sheets (also called transparencies) are placed over a light-box which is then magnified and projected on to the screen. The height of the projection can be altered, as can the clarity of the image. The transparencies can be prepared in advance by the speaker, or if, for example, asking for examples or comments from the audience, they can be written on during the talk using special fibre tip pens in an assortment of colours. Graphics can be produced onto acetate as well as text, and with the aid of a simple word processor and/or desk top publishing software professional-looking transparencies can be created.

The OHP needs to be located in front of the screen and cannot be operated remotely, therefore it can be distracting for the audience. An OHP is more commonly used in lecture/academic presentations where the style of delivery of the presentation is less critical. If using an OHP, a spare bulb is essential.

Slide projection

35 mm slides (also sometimes called transparencies) can be still photographs, drawings, diagrams, text, etc projected onto a screen either

- in front of the screen: front projection

- or from behind the screen: rear projection.

Rear projection looks neater as the projector does not need to be placed in the middle of the room, between the rows of seats, but it does require space behind the screen which can cut down the room's seating capacity. It is important to inform speakers if back projection is to be used as their slides will need to be loaded in the correct order but back to front.

Your options
- Using a **dissolve unit** makes it possible to use two projectors consecutively, allowing one image to fade out as another fades in, making for a very smooth transition.

- Other sophisticated techniques are also available and your AV technician will be able to discuss your requirements and advise on the options currently available.

- The projector can be operated manually or using cable or an infra-red remote control. The remote control allows the speaker to remain at his/her presentation point and move the slides on when required.

Types of slide
It is wise to encourage speakers to use glass-mounted slides if possible. Slides that are not glass-mounted can be affected by the heat of the lamp if the projector is in constant use and can also get caught in the projector. An argument is sometimes raised regarding glass mounts, that if dropped or damaged in transit the broken glass

can pierce the slide, damaging the slide irreparably. This is a valid point, but one that has to be weighed up against the same slide being damaged in the projector. Glass replacement slide mounts can be purchased in all good camera shops and it is possible to re-mount slides already produced using plastic mounts.

Other practicalities
It is useful for speakers to number their slides and to stick a coloured dot on the top of each one so that in the unfortunate case of a carousel being dropped (not an uncommon occurrence) they can be put back in the same order and up the correct way with ease.

'Blackout' (darkening of the room) will be essential for the slides to be effective. If using front projection the projector and stand will be placed between the rows of seats, the distance between the projector and screen being dictated by the size of image required and the size of the projector lens.

Video projection
Presenters may wish to use video footage to illustrate their talk. A television and a standard domestic video recorder would be unsuitable for any more than a very few delegates. The alternative is to use either a very large monitor, which may be impractical, a 'video wall' which could be costly, or to have the video feed plugged into a video/data projector so that the video image can be projected onto a normal screen.

This is often a costly exercise but worthwhile if the video really is a necessary part of the presentation. Sometimes a compromise can be made by running the video and monitor during the coffee breaks so that smaller groups can observe it. The presenter can then refer to relevant points during their presentation. Video tapes come in different formats (VHS, Super VHS, High-Band U-Matic or Betacam which is broadcast quality). Be sure that you ascertain the format and inform the supplier of the video equipment.

Computer generated graphics
Software is readily available which enables a presentation to be generated on a personal computer and then digitally projected onto a standard projection screen. The result can be extremely effective, and can include audio as well as visual effects. Photographs, text, diagrams and computer generated imagery can be combined to make interesting and memorable presentations. Unfortunately even more memorable is when such a presentation breaks down, and it is vital to

ensure that the technician or person in charge of the AV is aware of the version of software that has been used to create it. This is to ensure that the computer, leads and cables are compatible. It is also possible, and preferable, to transfer the presentation in advance on to a disk, CD Rom or email, so that it can be loaded onto the event computer that has been preloaded with the appropriate software.

Just in case the worst happens, it is advisable to have a back-up of the presentation on acetate or 35mm slides.

SOUND SYSTEMS AND RELATED ITEMS

Obviously it is essential that the delegates can hear the speakers. Be aware that the ability of sound to be absorbed and reflected means that the acoustics of an empty or full room will be quite different. **Ambient** (existing) noise, including the air conditioning unit if present, should be at a minimum, and the room should not be subject to external disturbances.

To ensure the speaker can be heard

Microphones
Through the use of a microphone an amplifier allows the volume of the speaker's voice/presentation aids to be adjusted to suitable levels. Some people who are generally softly spoken will be unable to project their voice very far without sounding like they are shouting, so it is essential that a sound system is in place.

Microphones can be hand-held, or more usually placed on an adjustable stand. They can also be placed on 'table-top' stands.

Radio and roving mikes
Some speakers, especially those who naturally tend to be more animated or who like to move around the stage, will be better suited to a radio mike which can be a tie-clip or hand-held microphone, which transmits the radio signal to the amplifier. In a similar way you could use the cordless radio or roving mike which can be passed around the audience at question time. As these microphones are battery powered, ensure you have spare batteries available.

A word of warning about using roving mikes – it is useful if one of your staff can 'control' its whereabouts as it passed around the audience so that any delegates with an axe to grind or someone who is going off at a tangent cannot get hold of it and refuse to let go.

Hiring equipment

Many purpose-built conference venues and hotels have amplifiers already situated in their conference rooms, and microphones can be hired from them at minimal cost. If, however, the room does not contain a sound system, check the cost of hiring one when evaluating the venue as the additional cost may be prohibitive.

Lecterns

A lectern is a stand for holding scripts, prompt cards, microphone, etc whilst the presenter is speaking. They come in an assortment of shapes and sizes, from a basic stand to one that contains a control panel for lights, the projector, the sound system, etc. They will usually have a light attached to illuminate the speaker's notes when the main lights are dimmed. It is useful to place a small, easily read clock on the lectern to enable the speaker to keep an eye on the time without having to look at his/her watch. If the lectern does contain a control panel ensure that the speakers and chairperson have been fully briefed as to its use.

If the venue cannot provide a suitable lectern an AV company will be able to supply one to suit your needs.

OPERATING THE EQUIPMENT

The AV technician (or operator) is an important player in the staging of an event. You need to decide who is going to take on the role. Options include one of your own staff or associates who has some knowledge of the systems being used. Alternatively you could use the services of a professional technician.

Choosing between professional and non-professional technicians

	Non-professional	*Professional technician*
• Benefits	Minimum cost	Professional charge (approx £150 per day)
		Experienced and quickly effective in case of breakdown
		Able to supply additional equipment as required

			Carries spare bulbs, batteries etc as required
			May be familiar with the venue
•	Drawbacks	May not be able to cope in breakdown situation	Financial implication
		If concentrating on equipment will not be able to participate in conference	
		Workload/stress during event will spoil person's enjoyment of the event.	

CONTRACTING AN AUDIO VISUAL COMPANY

Audio visual companies advertise their services in many trade magazines (see Further Reading) and can also be found locally in the *Yellow Pages*. Venue staff can also recommend local companies who are familiar with their venue.

It is worthwhile obtaining quotes from different AV companies before making a final decision, but be aware not to go by cost alone, experience is also very important. You are not only looking for a company who is within your budget (don't forget you could get sponsorship to cover the AV costs) but also someone who gives you the impression of being cool and effective in a crisis.

Audio visual companies can also provide stage sets, walk-in/ background music, lighting, autocues and more.

CASE STUDIES

Cassie tries to be cost conscious

Cassie is running a conference at a large city centre hotel. The speakers have fairly basic audio visual requirements, mainly consisting of 35mm slides. The venue has its own projector available to hire at a minimum cost. One of Cassie's colleagues, Ben, is a keen photographer with some experience of using a projector and has offered his services for the day (at least it will get him out of the office).

AUDIO VISUAL REQUIREMENTS FORM
to be returned by 20th April 199X

Speaker's Name:
Title of Presentation:
Date/Time:

I understand that my audio visual requirements as listed below will be provided. I also note that additional equipment will not be available unless previously specified.

Please tick...

35mm slides	☐
OHP	☐
Video	☐ specify exact format ....
Powerpoint	☐ specify exact version ....
	from your own laptop yes/no
	VGA/SVGA

Signed..

It is intended that, with your permission, the presentations will be recorded on audio tape and will then be available for purchase by delegates and other parties. Please confirm whether you give you consent for this to take place (*delete as appropriate*).

● I confirm that my presentation may be recorded and distributed.
● I do not wish for my presentation to be recorded and distributed.

Signed..

Fig. 16. Audio visual request form.

The great day arrives and the first two presentations go well, without a hitch. The third speaker opens his mouth to start his first sentence and his first slide jams in the projector. After some fiddling Ben manages to remove the offending slide, only for it to happen again... and again. The unfortunate speaker is becoming agitated as he is in the habit of using his slides as prompts for his dialogue. Ben is seriously stressed and thinks that the somewhat outdated projector may not have been serviced for some time. Just as things start to pick up again darkness falls upon the room. The bulb has gone and no one as a spare. Poor Ben, poor Cassie, poor speaker... and poor delegates.

Justine brings in the professionals

Justine is running a two-day conference for newly qualified accountants and is concerned that the assortment of audio visual technology that is to be used will cause problems by either breaking down or operator error. She discusses her concerns with the manager of an audio visual company recommended to her by the venue.

Justine and the manager talk through the programme and the AV requirements for each speaker. He supplies her with a quote to cover hire of equipment, delivery, installation and a technician to operate it. They do not need to do a site visit in this instance as he is very familiar with this particular venue. After a little negotiation Justine accepts the quote and the AV company completes the task well. The presentations are a success and everyone is happy.

9

Staging the Event

STAFFING THE EVENT

At the absolute minimum you will need at least one extra pair of hands at the registration desk in case you are called away to troubleshoot. The desk should be manned at all times throughout the registration period and afterwards in case of late comers.

A briefing to all staff members in advance of the first delegates arriving will ensure that they are aware of the location of toilets, cloakroom facilities and lunch room, and of time schedules and other important details.

Assessing staffing requirements

You will need adequate staff to make the day run smoothly. Before the event, ask yourself these questions:

- Who is going to switch the house lights on and off?

- Who is going to operate the projector?

- Who is going to pass around the roving mike?

- Who is going to deal with press enquiries?

If the conference is spread over a large campus, do you need directional staff at strategic points?

Meeting staff needs

If you do not have adequate staff readily available, you can often summon up help from various places. These could include:

- Local students if the venue is a university and the subject being discussed is appropriate to their area of study. Very often students, always on a tight budget, will appreciate free entry to the conference in exchange for tasks such as looking after the lights.

- Volunteers from your club/association.

- You can also hire professional conference staff from specialist agencies – obviously a costly option but worthwhile in terms of experience compared to the previous options. Agencies can be sourced from the trade shows/magazines listed in Useful Addresses and Further Reading.

Staff, whether voluntary or hired, must be smartly dressed in keeping with the image you wish to project. Badges will help delegates identify staff.

BEFORE THE DAY STARTS

Before anyone arrives walk the route from the car park or entrance to the registration desk and on to the conference room. Imagine you are arriving for the first time, as your delegates will be shortly. Is the route clearly signposted? Are there any recently-placed obstacles blocking the route? Is it clean and tidy? If the answer to any of these is no, sort out the problem immediately. This may mean doing it yourself or asking venue staff to take care of it.

Test (or witness) the audio visual equipment being used yourself to make sure all is working properly.

Briefing staff and delegates

Ensure that all key personnel are briefed in relation to evacuation procedures and any other related matters, and that the emergency exists are identified and kept clear. Their location and the congregation point outside the building should be clearly described to delegates during the chairperson's opening remarks.

DEALING WITH REGISTRATION

The registration desk should be sited where it is going to be easily spotted as delegates arrive, and where delegates are not able to slip through without registering. The desk should be kept free of junk – remember this is the first impression that delegates will have of the event. First impressions should not be underestimated. If you have access to display boards, two or three placed behind the desk will look professional, provide an opportunity to display the event or your organisation logo, and also provide somewhere behind which to store things.

If delegates are required to register and collect conference bags someone should be free to deal with queries which may arise, such as late payments, so as to avoid holding up the rest of the queue.

Often on your arrival you will be met by the venue co-ordinator who will run through the day's events with you. You should have the means to contact this person should a query or emergency arise during the event. This could be via walkie-talkie, phone or pager.

The purpose of badges

Badges are very useful for a number of reasons. As well as allowing immediate identification for security reasons they also encourage networking. For example, at an international conference very few people may know each other and placing the country of origin as well as the delegate's name on the badge can help to break the ice.

There are various options available. You can choose from a variety of materials including stickers, rigid plastic or the more common PVC badge holder with a card inserted into it. These come in a wide assortment of styles, sizes and prices. You can have badges pre-printed by a specialist badge company or you can print the delegates' names on labels and stick them onto a card printed with the event logo which can then be inserted into a badge holder.

Badge layouts
Depending on the type of conference, you can choose the layout that is most appropriate. At business events it is usual to include the delegate's name, position and company, but there are no hard and fast rules for this. Other ideas follows:

name	name	name	name
	company	post	company
		company	country

Badges can be attached to clothing by a pin or a clip. Ladies may prefer a pin as they typically do not have a breast pocket on suits. Tape **lanyards** are becoming increasingly popular allowing the delegates to hang the badge around their necks. The badges themselves and the neck cord offer another opportunity for sponsorship. The size of the font used on the badges must be large enough for the details to be read at a reasonable distance. This avoids delegates having to stand six inches away from the next delegate whilst staring at their bosom in order to read their name badge.

PREPARING DELEGATE PACKS

You may intend giving each delegate an information pack as they arrive. It may include a programme or itinerary, speaker biographies, abstracts of the presentations, a delegate list and any sponsored items such as pens, notebooks and advertising material. The pack may be a simple cardboard folder, a cloth bag, or even a small briefcase. The options are numerous and, of course, provide an excellent sponsorship opportunity. They should be packed in advance of the event as it can be a time-consuming and laborious job.

REMEMBERING DELEGATE CARE

You will want to create the best possible learning environment for your delegates, and that includes making them feel relaxed and welcome. Delegates who travel from some distance often overestimate how long it will take to get there, so expect them early.

You and your staff should remain helpful, cheerful and understanding throughout the event – but not patronising, especially if delegates arrive stressed after a difficult journey.

Coping with grievances

If a delegate has a grievance for any reason, take them away from the main registration area to discuss it. The benefits of this are:

1. You can give them your full attention.

2. They will feel you are listening to them.

3. Other delegates need not be affected by it.

Whether or not the complaint is justified, keep calm. Keep your voice steady and listen fully to what the person has to say. Obtain the facts of the matter, empathise with the complainant and assure them that you have understood their complaint. Be sure that any action promised to resolve the situation is taken and followed up as necessary.

In any situation where a query or grievance is made that cannot be dealt with immediately, assure the delegate that you will get the information or explanation they need as soon as possible (and don't forget to do it!)

Making registration smooth

Keep queues as short as possible. If the registration period is reasonably long you will find delegates arrive at varying times which makes the registration process much easier, as opposed to a 15-minute registration period for 200 people when they will all arrive at the same time. If delegate bags, papers, badges etc are to be issued, work out a system in advance so that it runs as smoothly as possible.

Providing an appropriate atmosphere
Providing coffee and tea during registration helps delegates to settle down after their journey before the conference starts and also helps to create a networking environment. Many venues include coffee on arrival in the day-delegate price – but do not take this for granted. Remember to check and order in advance if necessary.

Taking messages
It is useful to have a message board next to the registration desk. Telephone messages for delegates that come in during the day can be pinned on to it. You should be able to obtain the telephone number of the registration desk in advance of the event. If so, it can be useful to issue it to delegates in the confirmation letter, together with a reminder that mobile phones must be switched off whilst the conference is in session.

Contacting other services
Keep contact details for the local doctor, hospital, taxi and railway enquiry office in an accessible place as you will be bound to be asked for at least one of them. Also take along a tool box full of useful items, such as scissors and sellotape, that may be required.

Giving notice of time
If the day is going to run to schedule, it is essential that it starts on time. Give the delegates notice when the event is due to start, first ten minutes, then five minutes, then when it starts – there are always stragglers! When the delegates are all safely stowed in their room, tidy up the registration area in preparation for the morning break. Check the toilets to see if they are clean and tidy, and adequately stocked and alert the venue staff if they are not.

Looking after everyone
During the refreshment breaks, don't forget to look after those people who often get waylaid, such as the chairperson and the audio visual technicians. They will be as in need of refreshment as everyone else, but often find themselves tied up with delegates and other speakers.

ITEMS TO TAKE ALONG IN YOUR 'TOOL BOX'

- Velcro hoops
- Blu-tak
- Sellotape
- Masking tape
- Spare batteries
- Pencils and pens
- Rubber bands
- Cloakroom tickets
- Safety pins
- A needle and thread
- Drawing pins

- Tape measure
- Chalk
- A nail file
- Spare badge holders
- Scissors
- Staples and stapler
- Phonecards
- 10p coins
- Coins for parking meters
- A gentleman's tie
- Mints

Fig. 17. Tool box contents list.

Refreshment breaks

After the first refreshment break, assess how it went – were there long queues? Was there enough coffee? If there had been any problem alert the appropriate person (e.g. the hotel staff) so that the later refreshment breaks can be trouble-free. Waiting time for tea and coffee can be reduced by ensuring that the number of serving points are adequate for the number of delegates. One serving point for 150 delegates is going to result in considerably longer queues than three or four serving points. A useful tip is to have the milk sugar and biscuits on a separate table so that delegates move away from the serving area as swiftly as possible.

Lunch provision

If providing lunch for exhibitors, they will appreciate being able to have it prior to the delegates breaking for lunch. This must be pre-arranged with caterers and will result in stands being fully manned during breaks. The menu for lunch will have been decided upon some time before. If tables and chairs are not available in the lunch room, order a fork, or more preferably, a finger buffet so that delegates will be able to eat it easily. Most venues have a range of menus to suit a variety of budgets and seating arrangements and will be able to give advice based on their experience.

REMEMBERING SPEAKER CARE

Even experienced speakers can suffer from nerves before presenting, and this is no bad thing as the resulting increase in adrenalin often helps to boost the speaker's performance. There are certain steps, though, that can be taken to prevent the speakers becoming unnecessarily stressed. As mentioned in the chapter on choosing speakers, you should have provided the speakers with adequate directions to the venue and instructions as to what to do on arrival, such as whether they need to register with you and collect a badge, or whether they need to report to another person. If your budget and the facilities allow, it is useful to have a separate room for the speakers' use, where they can prepare themselves, run through their slides and generally get away from the hustle and bustle of the main conference area.

Before their talk is not the time to discuss payments and other details. Wait until after the presentation so that the speakers can remain focused on the job in hand.

Checking arrangements

- By requesting each speaker's estimated time of arrival and method of transport in advance you will be in a position to know whether there is any cause for concern if a speaker has not arrived at the start of the conference. Other commitments may prevent them from attending the whole event and you will expend much-needed energy and resources chasing missing speakers who may have had no intention of arriving until lunchtime for their afternoon talk.

- If visual aids are being used, introduce the speaker to the operator so that necessary information can be exchanged and time can be arranged for setting up their particular AV system.

- Don't forget the chairperson when dealing with speaker issues. Ensure they have been introduced to the day's speakers and that they have appropriate biographies to enable them to introduce them. They should also have a list of any 'housekeeping' notices they need to give, such as any health and safety instructions, lunch notices, etc.

- If you are in the luxurious position of having some or all of the speakers arriving for rehearsals prior to the event (perhaps whilst you are setting up the day before) allocate each of them a time slot so that they are aware that you will be working to a schedule. It is unfortunately not uncommon to set up a rehearsal afternoon and for all of the speakers to turn up expecting the technician's undivided attention during the final half-hour.

- A jug of fresh water should be available on or close to the lectern for the speakers and chairperson. One of the symptoms of nerves is a dry throat, so make sure that lubrication is within easy reach!

TROUBLE-SHOOTING

In the event of a disaster – the screen falls over, the sound system breaks down, a speaker fails to arrive – *stay calm*! Everyone will look to you for the answer; it is not the incident that will be remembered – it is how quickly you get things back together.

At the end of the day, don't forget to have a look around for any belongings that have been left behind by delegates. You will often find a jumper, an umbrella and someone's delegate bag containing their scrupulously taken notes. As the delegates are leaving all staff must be courteous and make the delegates feel that their presence has been appreciated.

Enjoying yourself

Above all, enjoy the event! Delegates, speakers and management will all take their cue from you as the key person. If you appear relaxed, cheerful but alert and ready to respond to any emergency, so will they. Conversely, if you appear nervous, anxious and look upon the whole event as a burden rather than a challenge, no one will enjoy it.

CASE STUDIES

Pamela finds a hole in the way

Pamela is running a conference at a university venue. By the time she reaches her bed on the evening before the conference everything is ready for registration the next morning. The delegates have been provided with a map to show them where to park and how to find the conference room on this large campus. In addition Pamela has clearly signposted the route from the car park to the conference room.

The next morning Pamela arrives early and awaits her delegates. When they finally start arriving they are flustered and irritated. Since Pamela's early arrival a team of water board officials has arrived and dug a hole in the main campus road to investigate a reported problem. This has resulted in vehicles being diverted around the campus and alternative car parks being put into use, leaving delegates wandering around in search of the conference room, with no signs to guide them.

Pamela makes a mental note to remind herself that next year she will ensure that the venue is signposted from all directions, just in case of unexpected holes or other diversions appearing on the anticipated route.

Jayne cools down a customer

Jayne is running a conference for businessmen and women on the increasing use of technology in today's offices. The conference is being supported by a small exhibition of suppliers of computer equipment and other technology. One delegate has arrived late as he had mislaid his directions and would rather be elsewhere today. He is generally on a 'short fuse'.

The session has just started but the delegate is not yet in a state of mind to take on board the information that is being given by the first speakers. Jayne has a few minutes break before she needs to get on with her next task. She offers to find the gentleman a cup of coffee and takes his overcoat. She listen patiently while he recounts each stage of his tiresome journey and watches him visibly unwind as he collects himself.

The gentleman then joins the other conference delegates, relaxed and eager to catch up on what he has missed. Jayne has had to find just a few minutes to make someone with the potential to be very negative, happy.

EXERCISE

Paying attention to detail is an essential element of event management. Here are a few small things that could make a big difference to the quality experienced by the delegates.

- Disposable paper cups instead of china crockery.
- Paper table covers instead of cloths.
- Handwritten directional notices instead of printed ones.

What others can you think of? Your final list will serve as a useful reminder when confirming exact requirements with venues.

10

Obtaining Press Coverage

THE PURPOSE OF MAINTAINING PRESS RELATIONS

Press coverage can be useful to:

- highlight particular topics of general interest
- encourage people to attend
- give an extra incentive to sponsors.

SELECTING THE APPROPRIATE MEDIA

Trade press
Specialist journals targeted at particular interest groups. These journals are often keen to include events which would appeal to their readers. They may also wish to send a representative along to write a report of the event in a later edition.

National press
Broadsheet and tabloid newspapers. The story needs to have strong general interest and be particularly topical. Many specialist supplements, such as the *Times Interface* (which is focused specifically on IT), have a regular 'What's On' listing and even if you cannot obtain any editorial space, if the subject is relevant you should not have any problem getting it listed.

Local press
Evening, daily, weekly and free papers. These papers focus on stories of interest to the local community and can be targeted from three angles as in the examples below.

Locality of delegates
'Local people are being encouraged to attend the West Cumbria Conservation Conference that is being held at the Diglis Sports Centre on 30th October. Many people relocate to West Cumbria

because of the beautiful countryside, but to secure its beauty for future generations we are all being encouraged to think ahead and to support schemes set up by the Conservation Trust that will be discussed...'

Locality of the event
'Bradshaw on Sea is delighted to be hosting the 1999 International Lacemaking Conference. The event, being run by the Bradshaw Lacemaking Circle, will attract delegates from across the world to hear speakers discussing the latest techniques and designs.'

Locality of speaker
'Dingford's Mayoress, Mrs Jean Smith, will be travelling to Cardiff on Saturday to address a conference aimed at reducing Local Government spending. Using Dingford as an example, Mrs Smith will discuss how smaller towns can flourish with creative spending.'

National radio

BBC and independent radio stations. As with national newspapers, the story needs to have strong appeal to catch the imagination of the radio producers/editors who will be inundated with press releases on a daily basis. By reading a copy of the *Radio* or *TV Times* it is easy to identify which programmes are devoted to particular issues – always send the press release to a particular show producer or editor, not just addressed to the radio station. A telephone call to the appropriate radio station is all that is needed to establish the programme producer's contact details.

Local radio

Local BBC and independent radio stations. Local radio, as local newspapers, need a continuance of stories about local people/issues, so try to target them from all three angles shown for local papers.

WRITING THE PRESS RELEASE

Remember that you are not only requiring the attention of the eventual newspaper readers, but that of the journalist him/herself who has to be persuaded to use the press release as a basis for an article. Editors and radio producers receive many press releases on a daily basis, so yours must stand out from the crowd. To do that you need a 'hook' to catch their attention.

Creating the copy

1. Ideally one A4 page should be adequate.

2. Many people will not read further than the first paragraph, so you have to be able to get your message across succinctly before going on to fill in the details in later paragraphs.

3. Type on one side of the paper only, use double line spacing, ensure it is dated at the top and has 'Ends' at the foot of the copy.

4. Under the main body of text put notes for the editor, such as contact name and telephone number for further details, enclosures etc. It may also be useful to note which, if any, of your speakers are 'media friendly', i.e. are comfortable, articulate and possibly experienced at talking to the media.

5. Include a quote from a spokesperson if appropriate.

6. Make the headline short and snappy, and avoid jargon and acronyms.

7. Include who, what, why and how.

8. Enclose photo(s) of speaker(s) and the conference brochure.

See Figure 18 for an example. Further details on writing a press release can be found in *How to Write a Press Release* (How To Books).

LOOKING AFTER THE JOURNALISTS

Always include details of how journalists can attend. Usually members of the press attend events free of charge, and in return publish articles on the conference. Ensure that they receive directions and instructions as to where to go on arrival. Remember that editorial space which journalists can provide would cost thousands of pounds if you had to pay for it in a national newspaper so it is a sound investment to put in the effort.

PROVIDING A PRESS ROOM

Depending on the profile of the event and if you are expecting high media interest, you may need to consider whether you will require a

PRESS RELEASE

Date: 5 May 199X

Capacity Crowd as Buxford Sports Club Goes for Gold!!

Over 150 people converged on the White Hart Hotel in Buxford at the weekend for a conference aimed at looking at how local sports clubs can contribute to the Government's on-going programme to create an abundance of world-class athletes to compete for the country at a professional level.

Delegates from sports clubs as far afield as Cornwall and Midlothian listened to speakers including the Sports Minister, the Right Hon Joe Bloggs (picture enclosed), who discussed the current situation and case studies of several projects that are running in some areas of the country.

Sponsored by Buxford's own Manglow Sports Superstore, the conference is set to become an annual event and next year the organisers are hoping to include a series of workshops and an exhibition to run alongside the conference.

'Buxford Sports Club should be proud of this initiative,' said an enthusiastic Mr Bloggs, 'with this sort of enthusiasm I am sure the new training programmes will soon be paying off and Britain will again be on the world map as far as athletics are concerned.'

Ends

Note for editors: For further details please contact Cathy Pritchard on 01234 56789. Enclosed: Photo of Rt Hon Joe Bloggs speaking at the 'Going for Gold' conference on 2nd May 199X

Fig. 18. Press release.

press room on-site for the duration of the conference. In here, you should provide any information that may be of interest to the media, including details of sponsors and exhibitors if appropriate. You should also provide:

- a phone
- fax machine
- coffee/refreshments
- seating.

If your budget will not stretch to a press room (remember to include room hire, phone charges, fax hire and refreshments in your budget), you can at least provide your press delegates with a folder including items pertaining to the cause of the event, biographies of speakers, literature from event sponsors and contact details for more information.

POST-CONFERENCE PUBLICITY

If you are unable to generate outside interest before and during the event, write your own review or press release afterwards for circulation to appropriate media. To add interest you can include quotes from satisfied delegates, and good quality photos of the conference in progress. As well as creating possible post-conference publicity, it will also alert the journalists to attend on another occasion.

EXERCISE

Study the papers that you/your office receives in one week. How many stories can you find that could have originated from a conference press release. Now write your own press release, making sure you have a strong 'hook'.

11

Exhibitors and Exhibitions

THE EXHIBITION INDUSTRY

The financial value of the exhibition industry is substantial. Exhibitions can be divided into **trade shows** and **consumer shows**:

- Trade shows are aimed at particular segments of industry or markets, such as the library industry or the security industry.

- Consumer shows are targeted at the end-user and as such are open to the general public, such as the Ideal Home Exhibition or the Boat Show.

Some exhibitions may run for several days, and have different days dedicated to the press, trade and the public. Stand-holders, or exhibitors, purchase space to display their wares or services alongside others. The exhibition companies provide the venue and facilities and aim to sell a required amount of exhibition space and to draw in as many visitors to the exhibition as possible to view those stands.

Becoming increasingly popular are consumer shows related to popular television programmes or magazines, such as The Clothes Show Live and the GQ ACTIVE Show. These enable members of the public to 'experience' the concept and participate in demonstrations, meet the presenters, etc.

Conferences and exhibitions

Large exhibitions are a separate part of the events industry and guidelines for running them are not within the scope of this book. However, many conferences do have exhibitors in one form or another to complement the conference, just as some exhibitions include a conference. In most cases the exhibition at a conference will consists of a handful of stands, some may have many more, but the emphasis is on the conference as the main event with exhibitors being welcome additions. However, the fact that the exhibition may be of secondary importance does not mean that it should be thrown together without due consideration and planning.

> Just as you would wish for the conference to be the best it could possibly be, the same should be true for the exhibition.

INCORPORATING AN EXHIBITION IN YOUR CONFERENCE

Why should we have exhibitors?

There are benefits to be gained by everyone if an exhibition is to be included in the conference agenda.

Benefits to the organisers
- Income generation from sale of stand space.

Benefits to the delegates
- Increased interest.
- Opportunity to talk directly to suppliers.

Benefits to the exhibitors
- Captive audience of potential customers.

SOURCING EXHIBITORS

As with sourcing potential sponsors, draw up a list of companies/ organisations which would identify your delegates as potential customers. It would be sensible for the option to exhibit to be included in the sponsorship form.

Having identified, contacted and reached an agreement with an exhibitor, confirm the arrangement in writing, detailing exactly what the package includes, what the cost will be and when the invoice will be issued.

WHAT TO INCLUDE IN THE COST

Some exhibitors use their own portable stands and will require only the space in which to erect it. However, this is by no means always the case and you should indicate whether furniture will be included, such as tables, cloths and chairs. As it is likely that these will be provided by the venue at no cost to yourself they should be included. Other furniture and display boards or shell schemes could be provided to order and invoiced for directly by the supplier.

Free delegate places to the actual conference will again not cost you anything other than the catering costs, so including a couple of places in the package will be seen as a benefit, and also make it clear that the places are limited and that it will not be possible for more stand staff to wander in and out as they please.

Shell schemes

Shell schemes can enhance the appearance of an exhibition by keeping the overall design of the stands the same. A combination of aluminium framework and panels of various materials, shell schemes can be supplied by specialist companies and can include a fascia board which allows company names and stand numbers to be displayed. Some panels are covered in a velcro-compatible loop nylon which allows graphics to be easily attached.

ALLOCATING SPACE

Obtain a detailed floor plan of the exhibition area, including power points and telephone points. Mark on potential exhibitor spaces. Look at where the premium sites may be. Delegates will tend to congregate:

- close to the coffee serving point

- immediately opposite the entrance to the exhibition

- on the main thoroughfares.

As exhibitors confirm their places the floor plan can also be confirmed and should be passed to the venue staff for approval. They will need to ensure that the layout meets with their Health and Safety requirements in terms of keeping emergency exits clear. The shell scheme contractors, if used, and anyone else involved in the construction of the exhibition stands, should be supplied with a copy of the floor plan.

Before the exhibitors arrive to set up, measure out the individual stand spaces and mark them up with chalk or masking tape. It may be that you are providing exhibition carpeting, in which case it may be possible to use a different colour carpeting for the stand areas to the rest of the floor.

The exhibitors should be provided with clear instructions and it can be helpful to provide them with an exhibitor pack or manual, similar to the speaker packs.

The exhibitor information pack

Background information on your organisation
They may be unfamiliar with the aims and objectives of your organisation and this will help them to understand 'where you are coming from'.

Overview of event
The aims and objectives of the event and a very brief history if it has run before.

Details of the exhibition
When it will run and the number and duration of the opportunities the delegates will have to visit the exhibition.

Details of the conference programme
They may have items that are pertinent to particular presentations.

Documents
1. What is required from them in terms of company description for the programme (including the maximum number of words to be used).

2. A form for the exhibitors to complete and return that confirms they will abide by all relevant Health and Safety requirements and that they have carried out a risk assessment in relation to their stand. This form must be returned before they arrive to set up their stand.

Clear directions/map
Easy to read and accurate. The directions should include location of loading bays and details of whether vehicles will be required to move to a particular parking area after unloading.

Details of what to do on arrival
Who to inform of their arrival. Include set-up times and dismantling times.

Delivery instructions
Details of where and when deliveries can be made before the event and from where collections can be made after the event. This should include details of names, departments, etc that should be clearly marked on packages. The venue staff will be able to advise you on this.

Details of lunch/hotel accommodation
Whether lunch/refreshments will be available for exhibitors and at
what cost if not complimentary.

Contact number for appropriate suppliers
Itemise exactly what will be available to them in terms of furniture –
tables, chairs, power points, etc – and give details of suppliers who
can provide additional items.

Parking pass
If applicable.

Contact details for queries
Details of how and when exhibitors can reach you, including on-site.

A feedback form
The opinion as to the success of the event is important from the
exhibitors' point of view as well as the delegates' and speakers', so
give them an opportunity to be constructively critical and to relate
their own experiences.

MAKING IT WORTHWHILE FOR EXHIBITORS

Conference exhibitors do not expect to have the attention of the
delegates throughout the whole event, but to make it worth their
while attending you must ensure that the delegates get to see them at
every opportunity. Refreshment breaks and the lunch period are the
most obvious. Refreshments should be taken in the exhibition area
so delegates are not drawn away from the exhibition. Nibbles and
sweet treats placed on the stands will help to encourage the delegates
to visit the stands. Perhaps you could serve a finger buffet in the
exhibition area and have dishes of scrumptious cakes and pastries
on the stands for dessert.

Delegates tend to disappear quickly at the end of the day, so if you
wish to encourage them to stay and view the stands again give them
some encouragement in terms of food and drink. You may be
thinking that all delegates do is eat and drink all day... but in fact
they do! It is part of the whole conference ethos and as an organiser
you will naturally segregate your day into feeding times.

Drawing attention to exhibitors

Instruct the chairperson to announce to the delegates when the exhibition will be open to them so that they have the opportunity to plan their visits to the stands. It will also help if you can spare a few minutes in the programme for a representative of each exhibiting company to introduce their company to the audience. Maximum use can then be made of the time available when delegates visit the stands. Just a couple of minutes each will suffice and help to make the exhibitors feel part of the event.

CASE STUDIES

Alistair finds some extra income

Alistair is running a conference on behalf of his local scuba diving club. The conference is aimed at divers from around the country and the purpose is to consider safety issues. It is a topical subject that has been discussed at length in the diving magazines and the club has been able to secure the services of a very well respected international speaker. The intention is to make the conference low cost for members of the National Association of Divers, to which most delegates will belong.

In order to increase the income Alistair decides to include a small exhibition and contacts suppliers of diving equipment to invite them to attend. The six suppliers who accept the offer pay £500 each, providing much needed cash to cover the international speaker's travelling expenses and accommodation. The delegates get the chance to talk to suppliers about their particular needs and can take advantage of many special offers that the exhibitors are offering.

Julie tempts the delegates with scrumptious snacks

Julie's conference consists of a seminar for all delegates in the morning who then split into groups for afternoon workshops. The delegates come together for all refreshment breaks and lunch. In order to encourage the delegates to visit the exhibition stands, Julie arranges for the buffet lunch, and the tea and coffee to be served in the exhibition area. Seating and round tables are scattered around the room encouraging delegates to spread out as much as possible.

In addition Julie hopes that some delegates will stay at the end of the conference to talk to exhibitors. To encourage this she arranges for trays of appetising cakes and pastries and glasses of punch to be placed on exhibitors' stands. The delegates have had an entertaining and informative day and now enjoy the opportunity to relax a little, partake of the food and drink and have a final chance to visit the exhibition stands.

EXERCISE

A well used tactic to encourage delegates to visit the exhibition stands is to place dishes of appetising treats on them. What else could you do to encourage delegates to visit the stands?

12

The Morning After

WINDING DOWN

After the busy period arranging and running the conference, it can be easy to lose the impetus to see the event through to the final stage. However, the days and weeks afterwards are very important as it is a time to analyse the conference and your own performance.

Ask yourself the following questions:

1. Did the conference satisfy the needs of the delegates?

2. Did the conference satisfy the needs of the organisers?

3. Did it serve its purpose?

3. Have the delegates taken on board what you wanted them to?

5. If they came to be educated, did they learn anything?

6. If they came to be informed, have they understood?

7. If they came to be entertained, have they gone away smiling?

8. Are the sponsors happy?

9. Are the exhibitors happy?

Newly formed relationships with delegates and sponsors can also now be consolidated, and post-event press coverage may be able to be obtained (see Chapter 10). Ensure that delegate details are passed on to those who may require them, such as sales and marketing departments, membership secretaries, etc.

DEVELOPING RELATIONSHIPS

Ensure you follow through any requests made by delegates during the conference. In readiness for this make sure that you take a full note of any requests at the time and put them somewhere safe where you are going to be able to find them again. A book specifically for this purpose is worthwhile.

Respond to any other queries that may follow promptly and courteously.

Remembering the speakers
Write to the speakers to thank them for their time and include payment for their services, expenses, etc if appropriate. Remember that the satisfaction, or not, of the delegates it largely in their hands and if it has worked out well they deserve to know about it. If you have used evaluation forms do pass on quotes to the speakers who may find them useful to use on other occasions.

Remembering the sponsors
Your agreement with your sponsors may have included a copy of the delegate contact details. If this is so, send them out promptly so that the company concerned can use them to their best advantage.

EVALUATING THE EVENT

Don't be afraid to ask delegates for their opinions on the event. By asking them complete a simple evaluation form at the end of the conference you can gather much useful information for future events, as well as obtaining their thoughts on your efforts this time around. The questionnaires can help you to make a judgement on the standard of venue, catering, booking arrangements, quality of presentations in content and delivery as well as obtaining suggestions for future events. See the example in Figure 19.

Designing an evaluation form
Include an easy to complete evaluation form in the delegate packs. Ask the chairperson to highlight their presence as you have a much greater chance of having a substantial and worthwhile number returned whilst still on site than posted or faxed back after they have returned home. Most delegates will be happy to take a few minutes to complete the form, after all it is in their best interests to do so as its purpose is to understand the needs of the delegates better for future events.

The use of tick boxes or a simple marking system wherever possible enables swift completion of the form. You may wish to include a grading system for each of the speakers, based on delivery and content. This can be particularly useful for future events, and speakers who have scored well are able to refer to it when being considered for other events.

You may wish to include the delegates' names and contact details, or you could make the forms anonymous (thus encouraging delegates to be rather more candid).

Diving for All Conference 199X

In order to provide the best possible service to our delegates, we would be very grateful if you would take a few minutes of your time today to fill in the following questionnaire. Please leave it in the questionnaire box by the desk or if you prefer fax (0234 45678) or post it back to us at Diving Today, PO Box 00, Bristol BS1 2UU.

1) Have you attended a Diving Today conference before? Yes/No

2) Did you learn of this one from (*please circle*)

Mailshot   Press   Word of mouth   WWW   Other

3) How would you grade the facilities at the venue? (*please circle*)

Poor   Adequate   Comfortable   Excellent

4) How would you grade the facilities at the venue? (*please circle*)

Poor   Average   Good   Excellent

5) Would you like to see future events held in (*please circle*)

Midlands   South   London   North   Scotland

6) Do you have any particular comments about this year's speaker programme?

7) Do you have any particular speakers in the UK or overseas you would like to hear at future events?

8) Are there any particular subject areas you would like to see covered at future events?

Thank you for your time.

Fig. 19. Evaluation form.

Professional research companies

Pre-event, on-site and post-event research can be undertaken on your behalf by professional marketing research companies using a variety of research methods. During the conference sophisticated and user-friendly terminals can be used that the delegates will be able to operate independently. Very useful data can be generated, and questions can also be included in the surveys on behalf of exhibitors, sponsors, etc. Professional reports will be provided that can be used to entice next year's exhibitors and delegates. An added benefit is that the research is seen to be unbiased as it is compiled externally. Specialist research companies advertise in trade journals and at trade exhibitions.

WHERE TO GO FROM HERE

Firstly, give yourself a pat on the back. Remember that everyone has different ideals and that to keep the entire range of people – from speakers, venue staff, delegates and the rest of your organisation – happy is no mean feat. As said in Chapter 1, a seamless event belies the amount of time and effort that will have been put in. All those who have contributed to its success should be made aware of the value of their input, and to this end a letter of thanks to them and/or their respective managers would be appreciated.

As a final thought, give some consideration to the following questions, and make a note of your answers while the subject is still fresh in your mind.

1. Are there things that you would do differently next time?

2. Are there alternative types of venue that would have been more suitable?

3. Did anything occur that you were not prepared for?

You will now be in an excellent position to run your next event. Reflect on what you have achieved since you began the project, the people who you have come into contact with. Ready to start again?

Appendix 1
Health and Safety

You are morally, legally and ethically obliged to ensure that everyone attending your conference will be safe. Organisers can be held responsible in cases of litigation and the penalties are severe. A thorough risk assessment should therefore be carried out in relation to the event.

CARRYING OUT THE RISK ASSESSMENT

You can do this yourself and advice can be obtained from your local Health and Safety Inspector. The Health and Safety Executive suggest **Five Steps to Risk Assessment**.

Step 1: Look for the hazards
A hazard is anything that can cause harm. Consider the venue, its physical surroundings, the staging and sets. Walk around the entire area where delegates, contractors, staff or speakers may have access.

Step 2: Decide who might be harmed and how
Consider everyone involved in the conference and how the hazards identified above could affect them.

Step 3: Evaluate
Evaluate the risks and decide whether the existing precautions are adequate or whether more should be done. A risk is the chance that somebody will be harmed by the hazard. How likely is it that each of the hazards identified in Step 1 could cause harm? Consider whether anything can be done to reduce the risk, to make it as low as possible. For example, if there is a step beyond a doorway that is not expected by someone walking through, a clear notice warning of it before the doorway will reduce the risk of someone falling down it. Although hazards may not be able to be completely eliminated, they can then be graded as being high, medium or low risk. Ask yourself these questions:

1. Can I get rid of the hazard completely?
2. If not, how can I control the risks?
   - try a less risky option if one is available
   - prevent access to the hazard
   - issue personal protective clothing/insist on contractors wearing necessary protective clothing.

Step 4: Record your findings

Keep a written record in your conference file and update it as necessary. In the instance of an investigation being made after an incident, the written audit trail will be vital evidence. A simple chart as in Figure 20 will also act as a prompt to ensure that the risk assessment has been completed. The chart should show that a proper check was made, by whom and when, that the outcome was that hazards were identified, people at risk were identified and that precautions have been taken to ensure risk is low.

Step 5: Review your assessment and revise if necessary

The level of risk and opportunities for hazards can alter as your conference progresses. Hazards may be present during the set-up day that are not present during the conference itself. Conversely the exhibition could add hazards that were not there before (see Chapter 12 – Exhibitors). It is vital then that the risk assessment is updated as significant changes occur. Also establish whether the venue has its own Health and Safety regulations that must be adhered to. Request these in writing and ensure they are built into your overall plan.

GETTING FURTHER GUIDANCE

The Health and Safety Executive publish a number of guidebooks to help you understand risk assessment and the legal requirements involved. Details can be obtained from: HSE Books, PO Box 1999, Sudbury, Suffolk CO10 6FS. The Five Step plan above is adapted from the HSE's publication *Five Steps to Risk Assessment.**

*Crown copyright is reproduced with the permission of the Controller of Her Majesty's Stationery Office.
This permission does not imply government endorsement of this product in preference to those of a similar nature which may be on the market.

Event title: *The Ages of Man*　　　　Date of event: *24th March 199X*

Organisation: College of Human Sciences　　Venue: *Tropador Museum*

Names of key personnel:　*Polly Marston (Organiser)*
　　　　　　　　　　　　Emily Marcus (Assistant to PM)
　　　　　　　　　　　　Anita Cork (Director - CHS)

Date of assessment: *12th March 199X*　Updated on: *23rd March 199X*

Assessment carried out by: *Polly Marston*

Hazards Identified	Level of Risk	People at Risk	Control/Action	Update/Notes
Electrical tools during exhibition set-up	*Medium*	*Exhibitors, other contractors*	*Ensure users are trained in their use. No such equipment is to be left unattended with a live power supply to it*	
Step down into gents toilet block easily missed	*High*	*All person entering the toilet block*	*Stick a thick line of contrasting tape along the edge of the step. Place warning sign at each side of the entrance*	*Draw to attention of venue management*
Injury from items related to exhibition break-down at end of conference	*Medium*	*All persons in immediate vicinity*	*Make sure exhibitors are issued with instructions not to break down their stands until all delegates have left the exhibition hall*	
Electrical and other cables in use by exhibitors, technicians etc	*High*	*All persons in locality*	*Trailing cables should be kept to a minimum and in protective sheaths. All to be taped down and secure and not trailing across walkways*	*Check all cabling before delegates are given access.*

Fire evacuation procedure established	Details issued to Chairperson	Details announced to attendees	Notes
Exits identified/ meeting place in safe area located as per instructions from venue	*24th March*	*During Opening remarks 24/3/9X*	*Briefing to all staff/ exhibitors not attending conference carried out by PM*

Fig. 20. Risk assessment form.

Appendix 2
First Aid

The Health and Safety (First Aid) Regulations 1981 require that first aid equipment, facilities and personnel trained in their use are provided in all places of work. This does not specifically include conferences, however the Health and Safety At Work Act 1974 requires that individuals have a duty of care to people who may enter our places of work. These may include conference delegates and contractors, but if there is any doubt it is better to err on the side of caution and have safety procedures in place as a matter of course.

According to the Health and Safety Executive, what is considered adequate and appropriate will depend on the circumstances. As a guide the minimum first aid provision on any work site is:

- a suitably stocked first aid box

- an appointed person to take charge of first aid arrangements.

An appointed person is someone who takes charge when someone falls ill, including calling an ambulance if required. The person should be available at all times, but should not attempt to give first aid for which they have not been trained. At all conferences there should be at least one qualified first-aider present, preferably one for every 50 delegates. A first-aider is someone who has undergone and holds a certificate from a HSE approved training course in first aid at work. The first-aider can also be the appointed person.

SUGGESTED MINIMUM REQUIREMENTS OF A FIRST AID BOX

- Twenty individually wrapped sterile adhesive dressings.

- Two sterile eye pads.

- Four individually wrapped triangular bandages.

- Six safety pins.

- Six medium-sized individually wrapped sterile unmedicated wound dressings.

- One pair of disposable gloves.

This information is taken from the excellent and very useful Health and Safety Executive web site. It contains question and answer pages, details of local contact numbers for enquiries, HSE statistics and an A–Z of relevant subjects. The site can be found at http://open.gov.uk/hse/hsehome.htm There is also an HSE InfoLine on 0541 545500, or you can write to: HSE Information Centre, Broad Lane, Sheffield S3 7HQ.

Appendix 3
Dealing with Committees

Conferences are frequently organised by societies, clubs and associations that are run by committees. The committee may appoint an individual to be in charge of organising the event on their behalf.

Committees are made up of a given number of individuals who fulfil a variety of functions. The committee members themselves will be an assortment of characters whose temperaments, beliefs, expectations, abilities and commitments will vary greatly.

ESTABLISHING CONTACT

The very fact that a committee is not an individual can result in prolonged decision-making and unnecessary complication of issues. It is therefore essential that you both (i.e. you and the committee) agree a point of contact through which you communicate with the committee and vice versa. That person can then be responsible for passing on messages through the committee, leaving you to get on with the organising. There are also positive points to a committee, for example you may discover that one or other of them has hidden talents or contacts that could be used.

Keeping them briefed

Committees like to be, and should be, informed of progress. Break down the organisation process into four stages:

- venue/date/budget, etc
- programme/speakers
- registration/site management
- de-brief.

You can then provide a succinct briefing document at each stage, updating them on key issues and pre-empting any questions they may have.

Making decisions

Before you start organising the conference, establish exactly what your boundaries are in terms of decision-making and responsibility. Ask the committee to provide this in writing if possible so that you both have a written contract/agreement. Having agreed the limits of your decision-making powers, establish how decisions outside your powers should be handled, e.g. to whom queries should be referred and how long decisions will take to be made. It may not be possible to await the next committee meeting, so forewarning the committee that this may occur will enable them to work out a system of their own.

Looking after the committee on the day

As the committee members will have been well briefed throughout the preparation stages of the event, they should all have a good understanding of how the conference is going to run. Ensure that any members with particular functions to perform, such as delivering a welcoming speech, are provided with any materials they may require.

Appendix 4
Booking Forms

As discussed in Chapter 4, the layout and design of the conference brochure are very important, it must not only look good, it must 'work'. Correct layout will ensure that when the delegate tears off and returns the booking form, essential information is not lost to them. The following diagrams (i) a suggested layout for a fairly simple booking system, and (ii) a more detailed example of the booking form section where various payment methods are included.

Front page

Title of Event

(Logo)

Date
Venue

Organisation

Sponsors' Logos

Back page

Venue Details

Written directions and/or map

The organisers reserve the right to substitute speakers/presentations if necessary

---

Detachable reply slip

Demographics

☐ ~   ☐ ~
☐ ~   ☐ ~
☐ ~   ☐ ~
☐ ~   ☐ ~

Special dietary requirements

....

Full names of delegates to appear on badges:

....
....
....
....

A simple booking form.

Detachable reply slip

Booking form
Title of Event

Name:
Address:

Tel: Fax: Email:

✂ - - - - - - - - - - - - -

I would like to book _____ ticket(s)
to attend the conference at

☐ £xx (Early Bird price)
   postmarked before xx/xx/xx

☐ £xx Standard price
   postmarked on or after xx/xx/xx

Please make cheques payable to
   Your company
Post to: Your name, Your company,
   Your address

Telephone no for enquiries (01234)
56789

Please complete both sides of form

Programme

Time Title of Presentation
Name of Speaker

"

"

"

"

Text

– Description
   of
Event

Booking form

Name............................

Postition........................   Organisation ....

Address: ....

....

.... Postcode ....

Telephone .... Fax .... Email......................

Special dietary requirements ....

Payment method

Cheque enclosed ☐   Credit card ☐
(payable to XXXX)   *(Visa/Mastercard/Delta)*

Credit card number............ Expiry date ....

Name of cardholder as printed on card ....

Cardholder's billing address *(if different from above)*................

....

....

Signature .... Total payment.....................

Post or fax your booking form to: Your Name, Your Company, Your Address, Your Postcode. Tel: (0123) 456789 Fax: (0123) 987654

Registration fees: Early Bird booking price £75 plus Vat
                       (postmarked before 11/05/00)

                       Standard booking price £85 plus Vat
                       (postmarked on or after 12/05/00)

Registration fee includes buffet lunch, tea and coffee, conference session and speaker papers where available.

A more complex booking form.

Appendix 5
Training Courses/Qualifications

Some trade associations run courses which are open to members and non-members. ACE (Association of Conferences and Events) regularly run two courses:

1. Principles of Meetings Planning.
2. Meetings Planning and Organisation (intermediate level/follow on to Principles of Meetings Planning).

These are residential courses covering three days and two nights, run in conjunction with the Meetings Forum. Further details from ACE on 01480 457595.

N/SVQs

National and Scottish Vocational Qualifications (NVQs and SVQs) are currently being developed. The Project Steering Group is composed of representatives of a multitude of event associations: ACE (Association of Conferences and Events), ABPCO (Association of British Professional Conference Organisers), AEO (Association of Exhibition Organisers), BECA (British Exhibition Contractors Association), EVA (Exhibition Venues Association), ITMA (Incentive Travel & Meetings Association), MIA (Meetings Industry Association), NEA (National Exhibitors Association), NOEA (National Outdoor Events Association), MUTA (Made-Up Textiles Association) and TESA (The Event Services Association).

Details regarding the progress of the Standards and N/SVQs are available from ACE on 01480 457595.

Several trade associations run seminars and workshops at various trade shows. Contact the shows on page 118 for details of their conference programmes.

It is also worth contacting your local technical college for details of any courses they may run that are relevant to the events industry.

Glossary

Ambient noise. Surrounding, existing, noise.

Audio visual. Sight and sound.

Autocue. A device displaying a script or prompt notes for a speaker's use.

Brainstorm. A meeting where spontaneous ideas are encouraged and nothing is dismissed until further discussion.

Break-even. The point at which income matches the fixed overheads so that no loss or profit is made.

Broadsheets. Full-size newspapers of more intellectual content than tabloids.

Call for papers. Announcement to interested parties that they may put forward ideas to be considered for inclusion in a conference programme.

Carousel. A removable tray in a projector which holds slides.

Chairperson. The man or woman who presides over a conference, acting as a master of ceremonies.

Delegates. The individuals who attend the conference, making up the audience. Also known as visitors or attendees.

Desktop publishing (DTP). The use of computer software to design and produce graphics, layouts etc.

Dissolve unit. A piece of audio visual equipment that enables projected images to gradually fade out/in.

Fixed costs. The costs incurred regardless of the number of delegates attending.

Fixed income. The income received regardless of the number of delegates attending.

Health and Safety Executive. A government body whose role is to ensure that risks to people's health and safety from work activities are properly controlled.

Lanyards. A cord which hangs around the neck to which a badge or other item may be attached.

Market research. The practice of gaining information about a given market.

Negotiation. To reach an agreement which may involve compromise by all parties.

Networking. The exchange of information, contacts, etc for mutual benefit.

Overhead projector (OHP). A piece of audio visual equipment that consists of a light-box over which acetate sheets are placed which are then projected onto a screen.

Registration system. The process through which delegate booking data is organised.

Risk assessment. The systematic assessment of risk of injury to persons in the vicinity of the conference.

Software packages. Operating programs used on a computer.

Tabloids. A popular newspaper of half-size pages (as opposed to a broadsheet newspaper).

Time plan. A systematic plan drawn up with the intention of making best use of available time.

Variable costs. Those costs which may vary according to number of delegates in attendance.

Variable income. The income that will be generated according to the number of delegates who attend.

Further Reading

TRADE PUBLICATIONS

Conference & Exhibition Fact Finder (Batiste Publications Ltd. Tel: (0181) 340 3191).

Event Organiser (Trade Publications. Tel: (01235) 821820).

Exhibition Bulletin Yearbook (Exhibition Bulletin. Tel: (0181) 778 2288).

Meetings and Incentive Travel (Conference and Travel Publications Ltd. Tel: (01342) 824044).

Meeting Planner (Hallmark Communications. Tel: (01273) 691113).

Who's Who in Exhibitions? (Who's Who in Exhibitions? Ltd. Tel: (0181) 516 3010/3291).

Who's Who in the Meetings Industry (The Annual Yearbook of the Association of Conferences and Events. Tel: (0171) 976 1977).

Useful Addresses

Association of Conferences and Events, ACE International, Riverside House, High Street, Huntingdon, Cambridgeshire PE18 6SG. Tel: (01480) 457595. Fax: (01480) 412863.

Association of Exhibition Organisers, 26 Chapter Street, London SW1P 4ND. Tel: (0171) 932 0252. Fax: (0171) 932 0299.

Association of Independent Tour Operators, 133a St Margaret's Road, Twickenham, Middlesex TW1 1RG. Tel: (0181) 744 9280. Fax: (0181) 744 3187.

Association of National Tourist Office Representatives, 211 Piccadilly, London W1V 9LD. Tel: (0171) 917 9536. Fax: (0171) 917 9537.

British Association of Conference Destinations, 1st Floor, Elizabeth House, 22 Suffolk Street, Queensway, Birmingham B1 1LS. Tel: (0121) 616 1400. Fax: (0121) 636 1364.

British Exhibition Contractors Association, 36 The Broadway, Wimbledon, London SW19 3SR. Tel: (0181) 543 3888. Fax: (0181) 543 4036.

British Hospitality Association, Queens House, 55–56 Lincoln's Inn Field, London WC2A 3BH. Tel: (0171) 404 7744. Fax: (0171) 404 7799.

British Universities Accommodation Consortium, University Park, Nottingham NG7 2RD. Tel: (0115) 950 4571. Fax: (0115) 942 2505.

Connect Venues, Higher Education Accommodation Consortium, The Work Station, 15 Paternoster, Sheffield S1 2BX. Tel: (0114) 249 3090. Fax: (0114) 249 3091.

Corporate Hospitality & Event Association, Arena House, 66–68 Pentonville Road, Islington, London N1 9HS.

Events Sector Industry Training Organisation, Riverside House, High Street, Huntingdon, Cambridgeshire PE18 6SG.

Exhibition Venues Association, Mallards, Five Ashes, Mayfield, East Sussex TN20 6NN. Tel: (01435) 872244. Fax: (01435) 872696.

Incentive Travel & Meetings Association, PO Box 195, Twickenham, Middlesex TW1 2PE. Tel: (0181) 892 0256. Fax: (0181) 891 3855.

Meetings Industry Association, 34 High Street, Broadway, Worcestershire WR12 7DT. Tel: (01386) 858572. Fax: (01386) 858986.

Society of Event Organisers, 29a Market Square, Biggleswade, Bedfordshire SG18 8AQ. Tel: (01767) 316255. Fax: (01767) 316430.

TESA, The Event Services Association, 8 Home Farm, Ardington, Oxfordshire OX12 8PN. Tel: (01253) 821820. Fax: (01235) 862200.

The Tourism Society, 26 Chapter Street, London SW1P 4ND. Tel: (0171) 834 0461. Fax: (0171) 932 0238.

TRADE SHOWS

BUAC Show (London), British Universities Consortium. Tel (0115) 950 4570.

Business to Business Exhibition (Manchester). Tel: (0113) 237 3022.

Confer (London), British Association of Conference Destinations. Tel: (0121) 616 1400.

Confex, The Meetings and Events Exhibition (London), Miller Freeman. Tel (0181) 742 2828.

Convene (Manchester). Tel: (01440) 820173.

The Event Show (London), Inside Communications Ltd. Tel: (01203) 230333.

Incentive (London), Miller Freeman. Tel (0181) 742 2828.

Incentive World (Wembley), Avenue Exhibitions. Tel: (01273) 325455.

Meetings and Incentive Travel Show (London). Tel: (01342) 824044.

ShowExpo (London). Tel: (01252) 811163.

Index

CONDUCTING STAFF APPRAISALS
A practical handbook for every manager today

Nigel Hunt

This book, now in a third edition, sets out a basic framework which every manager can use or adapt, whether in business and industry, transport, education, health or public services. Nigel Hunt is a consultant in occupational testing, selection, appraisal, vocational assessment, and management development. He is a Graduate Member of the British Psychological Society, and Associate Member of the Institute of Personnel & Development. 'Informative. . . points for discussion and case studies are prominent throughout. . . the case studies are highly relevant and good.' *Progress* (NEBS Management Association Journal). 'Not all books live up to their promises. This one does. At the price it is a bargain.' *British Journal of Administrative Management.*

154pp. illus. 1 85703 399 X. 3rd edition.

WINNING PRESENTATIONS
How to sell your ideas and yourself

Ghassan Hasbani

No matter who you are or what kind of work you do, you always need to communicate with people on different occasions and present to them ideas, news or achievements. This step-by-step guide tells you all you need to know in order to become confident in giving effective presentations, which will help you succeed in your life and career. Ghassan Hasbani currently works as a Senior Marketing Specialist, where he uses his skills to present new technologies in seminars and lectures.

154pp. illus. 1 85703 309 4.

MANAGING YOURSELF
How to achieve your personal goals at work

Julie-Ann Amos

Managing yourself is often more difficult than it seems. This simple book goes beyond assertiveness and behaviour, and examines how to deal inside ourselves with the conflicts of everyday life. The reader will learn how to handle criticism, thoughts and emotions, aggression, passivity, change, conflict, and stress, through developing assertive communication and listening skills, body language and confidence.

160pp. illus. 1 85703 324 8.

MANAGING THROUGH PEOPLE
How to get the best from your most valuable resource

John Humphries

People are the most valuable resource of any organisation, and managing people successfully is the surest way for an organisation to achieve its objectives. *Managing Through People*, originally titled *How To Manage People at Work*, has been fully revised to take into account the changing role of managers, for example how to support and coordinate a non-standard workforce, such as those working from home on a freelance basis. In fact this book covers, in one handy volume, every aspect of people management that today's business leaders require. 'Highly informative, reliable, comprehensive and user-friendly – has tackled an extremely wide subject ably and well.' *Progress* (NEBS Management Association). John Humphries BSc has 20 years' professional experience as a management trainer and is an NVQ assessor.

128pp. illus. 1 85703 271 3rd edition

MANAGING SUCCESSFUL TEAMS
How to achieve your objectives by working effectively with others

John Humphries

A team is a collection of individuals with their own ideas and abilities but with the willingness to share their ideas and use their abilities to achieve a common objective. It is generally recognised, therefore, that teams operate more effectively and efficiently than groups of individuals. This book is designed to help anyone who has the task of building and leading a team. It is full of sound, practical advice and contains a large selection of exercises that you can organise and run. John Humphries is a management trainer with over 20 years' experience of training people, both in the UK and abroad. He has written three other books in this series, including the very successful *Managing Through People*.

144pp. illus. 1 85703 282 9.

WRITING A REPORT
A step-by-step guide to effective report writing

John Bowden

Written by an experienced manager and staff trainer, this well-presented handbook provides a clear step-by-step framework for every individual, whether dealing with professional colleagues, customers, clients, suppliers or junior or senior staff. Contents include: preparation and planning, collecting and handling information, writing the report, improving your thinking and presentation, achieving a good writing style, making effective use of English, and how to choose illustrations, paper, covers and binding. 'Thoroughly commendable.' *IPS Journal.* John Bowden MSc has long experience both as a professional manager in industry, and as a Senior Lecturer running courses in accountancy, auditing and effective communication.

215pp. illus. 1 85703 285 3. 4th edition

MANAGING YOUR TIME
What to do and how to do it in order to do more

Julie-Ann Amos

Time cannot be managed. It can't be increased, delegated, reallocated, saved, or lost. What you can manage is the way you use time. This practical guide looks at the two issues of what you do and how you do it. Doing the right things in the best way means we can use our time to our best advantage efficiently. You will learn the difference between efficiency and effectiveness, and how to use them to make time your friend, not your enemy. Julie-Ann Amos BSc holds postgraduate qualifications and memberships of the Institutes of Personnel Development and Administrative Management. She works as a human resources consultant with a number of public and private sector companies.

144pp. illus. 1 85703 288 8.

MAKING EFFECTIVE SPEECHES
How to motivate and persuade in every business situation

John Bowden

Written specifically for people competing in today's tough business world, this book shows you how to get that competitive edge by becoming a comfortable, effective speaker, equipped with the skills necessary to deliver dynamic business speeches. You will learn how to communicate your ideas, motivate employees, influence opinions, and much more. Business speeches are important – they must succeed. This book will help turn your speeches into personal and corporate triumphs. John Bowden MSc has over 25 years' experience as a manager in industry, and as a professional trainer and senior lecturer in communication skills. He is author of *Making a Wedding Speech* and *Writing a Report* in this series.

144pp. 1 85703 291 8.